FALLING FRIENDS

The United States
and Regime Change Abroad

Titles in This Series

Falling Friends: The United States and Regime Change Abroad,
edited by Martin Staniland

FORTHCOMING

Ethics and International Affairs,
edited by Rachel M. McCleary

Negotiating for Peace, edited by Allan E. Goodman

Multilateral Negotiations, edited by Abiodun Williams

*International Financial Negotiations: Global Debt
and Structural Adjustment in Comparative Perspective,*
edited by Thomas J. Biersteker

Case Studies in International Affairs
Series Editor: Martin Staniland, University of Pittsburgh

The case-study approach to teaching and learning is on the rise in foreign policy and international studies classrooms. Westview Press is pleased to promote this trend by publishing a series of casebooks for a variety of college courses.

Innovative educators are using case studies to:

- Develop critical thinking skills
- Engage students in decisionmaking and role playing
- Transform lecture courses into interactive courses
- Encourage students to apply theoretical concepts using practical experience and knowledge
- Exercise skills in negotiation, management, and leadership

Each book will include theoretical and historical background material, four to eight case studies from all regions of the world, material introducing and connecting the cases, and discussion questions. Teaching notes will be provided to adopting professors and, to encourage the use of several different books and themes within a single class, the casebooks will be short, inexpensive paperbacks of approximately 150 pages.

The individual case studies making up the heart of each volume were developed in conjunction with seven institutions—University of Pittsburgh, Harvard University, Georgetown University, Columbia University, Johns Hopkins University, University of Southern California, and the International Peace Academy—under the auspices of The Pew Charitable Trusts. From over 140 case studies developed by leading scholars, the editors have selected those studies that thematically and substantively offer the best classroom examples for each topic in the series.

FALLING FRIENDS

The United States
and Regime Change Abroad

edited by

MARTIN STANILAND
University of Pittsburgh

Westview Press
BOULDER ■ SAN FRANCISCO ■ OXFORD

Case Studies in International Affairs

This volume, as compiled, copyright © 1991 by Westview Press, Inc. The following case studies have been edited and are reprinted here with permission: "The United States and the Cuban Revolution, 1958–1960" by Pamela K. Starr and Abraham F. Lowenthal (Pew case study no. 328) copyright © by The Pew Charitable Trusts; "Nicaragua, 1978–1979: The United States and Anastasio Somoza—Dealing with Friendly Dictators Who Are Losing Their Authority" by Douglas A. Chalmers (Pew case study no. 105) copyright © by The Pew Charitable Trusts; "The United States and Nicaragua: Anatomy of a Failed Negotiation for Regime Change, 1977–1979" by Alex Roberto Hybel (Pew case study no. 327) copyright © by The Pew Charitable Trusts; "The Ethics of Intervention: The United States and Nicaragua" by Rachel McCleary (Pew case study no. 347) copyright © by The Pew Charitable Trusts; "The Fall of the Shah of Iran" by Gregory Treverton with James Klocke (Pew case study no. 311) copyright © by The Pew Charitable Trusts, the University of Pittsburgh, and the President and Fellows of Harvard College; "The Iranian Hostage Negotiations, November 1979–January 1981" by Andrew Steigman (Pew case study no. 348) copyright © by The Pew Charitable Trusts; "The Fall of Marcos" by William E. Kline (Pew case study no. 439) copyright © by The Pew Charitable Trusts, the University of Pittsburgh, and the President and Fellows of Harvard College; "US Policy Concerning Renewal of the Military Base Agreement with the Philippines" by Donald M. Goldstein (Pew case study no. 325) copyright © by The Pew Charitable Trusts; "To Save the Philippine Republic: The Decision to Reform the Government of the Philippines, 1949–1951" by Douglas J. Macdonald (Pew case study no. 440) copyright © by The Pew Charitable Trusts; "Political Crisis and Debt Negotiations: The Case of the Philippines, 1983–1986" by Penelope Walker (Pew case study no. 133) copyright © by The Pew Charitable Trusts.

Published in 1991 in the United States of America by Westview Press, Inc., 5500 Central Avenue, Boulder, Colorado 80301, and in the United Kingdom by Westview Press, 36 Lonsdale Road, Oxford OX2 7EW

Library of Congress Cataloging-in-Publication Data
Falling Friends : the United States and regime change abroad / edited
   by Martin Staniland
      p. cm.—(Case studies in international affairs)
   Includes bibliographical references.
   ISBN 0-8133-8259-9 (hard)—ISBN 0-8133-8260-2 (pbk.)
   1. United States—Foreign relations—1945-   . 2. Political
stability—History—20th century.   3. World politics—1945-
I. Staniland, Martin. II. Series.
E840.F28 1991
327.73—dc20   90-24293
                                                                           CIP

Printed and bound in the United States of America

The paper used in this publication meets the requirements of the American National Standard for Permanence of Paper for Printed Library Materials Z39.48-1984.

10   9   8   7   6   5   4   3   2   1

To Paul, Laura, and the R.R.R.R.

CONTENTS

PREFACE

The Westview series "Case Studies in International Affairs" stems from a major project of The Pew Charitable Trusts entitled "the Pew Diplomatic Initiative." Launched in 1985, this project has sought to improve the teaching and practice of negotiation through adoption of the case-method of teaching, principally in professional schools of international affairs in the United States.

By 1989, authors associated with the seven institutions involved in the Diplomatic Initiative had written over 140 case studies in international negotiation for classroom use.[1] In considering a second phase of the program, The Pew Charitable Trusts determined that its emphasis should shift from writing cases to encouraging their adoption in courses taught through the case-method.

One aspect of this phase has been the establishment of a clearinghouse at the Graduate School of Public and International Affairs, University of Pittsburgh, to distribute and promote the cases. During the first two years of the clearinghouse's operation, it quickly became clear that a sizeable market for the case studies (and a considerable interest in case-method teaching) existed in the larger community of university and college undergraduate instruction. By October 1990, over 15,000 single copies of cases had been sold, and the circle of customers had widened to include instructors in such countries as India, Bulgaria, and the Soviet Union.

It also became clear that, although a classroom use for individual cases would always exist, there was instructional potential in sets of cases selected to illustrate particular issues in negotiation as well as negotiations over particular policy matters. Hence the Westview series, which offers students and instructors the opportunity to examine and discuss specific themes, including themes (such as foreign policymaking) that fall outside of the ambit of international negotiation. Each volume presents a selection of cases, some short, others long, some essentially unchanged, others extensively edited or rewritten. Each volume also contains an introductory chapter, identifying the characteristic features and dilemmas of the kind of negotiation or issue exemplified by the cases. Each volume contains questions for discussion, suggestions for simulation, and further reading.

Case-method teaching typically involves two elements. The first (and essential) element is careful reading of a case document by students. The second is one or more classroom sessions in which an instructor, using sustained Socratic questioning, tries to get students to explore the meaning of events that are described, but deliberately not interpreted or explained, in the case document.

Like all teaching, case-method teaching depends on a contract, however implicit. The contract here is framed by two norms: the first is that the material within the case provides a common stock of evidence and an obligatory point of reference. If this norm is broken by the introduction of extraneous or privileged information, the case will cease to serve as a common focus, the assumption of equal information (however artificial and fictitious it may be) will break down, and some students will feel discouraged from participating.

The second norm is one of judgmental equality--that, for purposes of the discussion, the instructor willingly suspends his or her authority for the sake of encouraging students to develop and express their own interpretations of events. Although the instructor may (indeed, should) organize discussions so as to lead students into specific questions, he or she will undermine the exploratory and interactive character of the discussions if students have the impression that they are required to discover "the right answers." This does not mean that instructors have to say (much less to believe) that they have no opinions or that one person's opinion is as good as another's. It simply means that they should be prepared to retreat, temporarily, to the roles of agenda-setter and discussion leader, rather than assuming those of decisionmaker and interpreter.

Although obviously there are some important premises regarding educational philosophy and psychology underpinning belief in case-method teaching, the case for instructors holding back is essentially pragmatic--that discussion is a good educational vehicle and that students will only climb onto it if they are allowed to share in the driving.

Case-method teaching is, then, a tool, supplementing the conventional tools of exposition. Cases can be used to follow up lectures; they can (as this series implies) be used comparatively; they can be used for discussion or for simulation. They can be used with or without accompanying writing assignments. They can be used to illustrate theoretical concepts (such as power) or to require students to enter into the agonies of political choice ("What would you have done if you were President Carter?") But what they invariably do is to enable--and to force--students to take responsibility for their own political and academic education. The faint burning smell of hard thinking hangs in the air after a good case discussion has taken place. Surely anything that produces that smell should be welcome.

Martin Staniland
Series Editor

NOTES

1. The institutions concerned were the School of International Relations, University of Southern California; the School of International and Public Affairs, Columbia University; the Edmund A. Walsh School of Foreign Service, Georgetown University; the John F. Kennedy School of Government, Harvard University; the International Peace Academy (of the United Nations); the Paul H. Nitze School of Advanced International Studies, Johns Hopkins University; and the Graduate School of Public and International Affairs, University of Pittsburgh.

ACKNOWLEDGMENTS

I am most grateful to two people who have shaped and sustained this volume--and the series to which it belongs--from the beginning. One is Jennifer Knerr of Westview Press, who has provided the essential publisher's nutrients--consistent encouragement and continual enthusiasm. The other is Kendall Stanley, coordinator of the clearinghouse and WordPerfect wizard, without whose skill and dedication there would not even be cases. There would also be no cases (and no series) without the support of The Pew Charitable Trusts: I especially thank Jim McGann and Kevin Quigley for supporting the idea of a book series and for allowing us to edit and reprint the cases.

For their help in this and innumerable other matters over the past six years, I want to thank my "colleagues-in-Pew": Tom Biersteker, Steve Lamy, and John Odell at USC; Steve Cohen and Graham Irwin at Columbia; Jim Goodby, Allan Goodman, and David Newsom at Georgetown; John Boehrer and Peter Zimmerman at Harvard; Bill Zartman at SAIS; and Chris Coleman and Tom Weiss at IPA. For some extended and very helpful comments on the proposal for this volume and a possible follow-up book, I am grateful to Davis Bobrow, a dean and yet still cheerful. Most of all, I want to thank Alberta for all her listening and even for some of her criticisms.

M. S.

1

INTRODUCTION

Nicaragua was a client-state of the United States. This term refers to an alliance between states that have vastly different resources and power. The dominant power provides its client with protection from external and internal enemies; in synthesis, it supports the local government. In exchange, the client provides special services to its patron, such as economic privileges and political and military services.[1]

One morning in the mid-1950s, a BBC announcer reported, concerning one of the frequent colonial crises of the time, that the British colonial secretary was flying off to East Africa on a "fact-facing mission." This Freudian slip no doubt reflected exactly, if unintentionally, what was happening. The moment for such a mission, physical or intellectual, comes in all the crises described in this volume. At this point, the unthinkable is not only thought, but said--that a regime to which a major foreign power has become deeply committed is about to fall and is beyond help.

This volume deals with the diplomatic problems involved in this kind of crisis. The cases included in the volume refer to episodes in which the foreign power in question is the United States, but clearly a similar series of crises has afflicted the Soviet Union, particularly within the last three years.

Comparative studies of regime succession are rewarding for several reasons. They enable us to see several elements of foreign policymaking under the bright and harsh light of crisis. Alliances among policymakers are likely to come under strain, and divisions are likely to open up. Intelligence becomes of great importance, both in the gathering and in the interpretation. Sharp questions and urgent doubts arise. Do we really know what is happening? Can we be sure that soundly based assessments are reaching policymakers (and are being digested)?

Relations between diplomats in the field and their superiors at home are likely to be tested. Can we trust the ambassador to understand (and respect) instructions from home? Can we be confident that he or she is sufficiently detached from the imperiled regime to be able to give hard-headed assessments of its prospects as well as good advice about policy toward it?

A crisis also illuminates the "policy network" attached to the foreign relationship in question. Within a short time, newspaper readers and TV viewers will become all too familiar with representatives of immigrant groups, leaders of exiled political groups, relevant State Department and other officials, interested members of Congress, and people with business interests in the area. In addition, they will develop an unexpected acquaintance with the inevitable academic and think-tank experts, enjoying (it is obvious) a mass celebrity, which is likely to be short-lived, surviving only until "their" country disappears again from the consciousness of the media managers.

WEAK STATES OR DEPENDENT STATES?

Succession crises are also revealing in a more fundamental way. They provide a crucial moment when the foundation of the relationship between patron and client is exposed and, indeed, may be shaken (as in the Cuban, Nicaraguan, and Iranian cases). As Bruce E. Moon has argued, the power of a strong state relative to weaker states is expressed not so much in a capacity to enforce compliance over particular issues as in a longer-term ability to shape the society and the regimes that govern it.[2] To demonstrate the ability of a stronger country to influence individual decisions of a weaker one (for example, over how to vote at the UN) requires showing that the regime influenced would, if left alone, have taken a decision different from that preferred by the patron. Not only is this hard to prove, but it may be that apparent "compliance" (presumed to be the result of pressure by the stronger state) actually reflects a consensus.

No enduring authority or influence in fact rests on a continual series of confrontations and bargains. Rather, the weaker party acquires a sense of the inherent, even natural, rightness of the superior. Authority is grounded in cultural borrowings: Power is acknowledged as much through memories of its past exercise as through daily demonstrations. In all the cases used here, observers commented on how complex and intimate the relationship between the United States and the society conconcerned had become. Behind the apparently straightforward ideological and diplomatic oppositions played out center stage, some murkier and often contrary movements could be glimpsed. Radical anti-Americanism often seemed to rest on some (to Americans) flattering, excessive, and even mystical notions about the ubiquity and tenacity of American power--notions that could only have survived in societies much more penetrated, at least at middle-class level, by American values than the nationalists publicly acknowledged (or perhaps understood). The Philippines presents the clearest example of pervasive acculturation. But even after the Sandinista revolution, baseball continued to be both Cuba's and Nicaragua's national sport, and the Ortegas were known to enjoy shopping in Manhattan.

Yet it is dangerous simply to label such states as "dependent." The term itself has confusing and misleading psychological associations. There is no question that societies such as the Philippines or Cuba have been subject to enormous influence by the United States. Indeed, "dependency" may well be a good term to describe the behavior and thought processes of members of the elite. Properly speaking, too, the terms *patron* and *client* apply to governments--to people--rather than to states.

It is confusing and, in fact, unnecessary to apply an essentially behavioral and psychological term to a state. All that is necessary is to show how the exercise of the sovereignty that the state formally enjoys is limited by military, diplomatic, economic, and cultural influences emanating from the hegemonic power. If we emphasize constraints when examining the situation of the state, we avoid the over-deterministic position to which some dependency theory leads, from which it is very difficult to explain cases of apparent, albeit temporary or illusory, breakout, such as Cuba and Nicaragua.[3]

Referring to *strong* and *weak* states is surely better. Even if such terminology raises problems of its own, at least it focuses attention on a recognizable and appropriately political world of greater and lesser risks, opportunities, costs, and benefits. If, in addition, we can show that, through training, habit, or experience members of the society are disposed to minimize opportunities for independent action by the state or to disparage the prospective benefits of such action, so much the better. In the apt phrase of the authors of the Cuban case, they may be gripped by a sense of "geographic fatalism."

To separate conventionally political and behavioral categories in this way is also helpful in understanding why, among states that seem objectively to be equally weak, some may act more assertively than others. We might reach a startlingly simple conclusion, namely, that the only really "dependent" states are those whose leaders believe they are. The rest may be weak, but weakness can be parlayed into something curiously resembling strength by astute and self-confident leaders.

In fact, we have only to look at American behavior in some of the cases used here to see both how simplistic a division into "dominant" and "dependent" states is and how complex the actual relationships are. American behavior, in its contradictions and hesitations, exhibits all the paradoxes and ambivalences of a society caught up in (rather than simply dictating) the history of others. Despite the obvious predominance of American power and much talk of "American national interest," none of the transitions described here was effected (or affected) by the dispatch of American forces. In fact, much of the action took place within a restricted circle of long-time acquaintances, and as much in Washington as in the foreign capital concerned.

Indeed, it is often a question (with, for example, Somoza and especially the Marcoses) who is patron and who client, so skilled and confident are the supposed "puppets" in penetrating the inner circles of influence in Washington. Such skill came not from distant study or good intelligence services, but from a deep personal comfort and acquaintance with American institutions and folkways. Such intimacy explains also the sometimes dangerously personal cast of many of the relationships observable here--"dangerous" to the extent that protection of admittedly more abstract foreign policy interests became entangled and confused with the mutual and often emotionally charged commitments of individual leaders.

The general point is that both the economic and the normal exercise of "power" in relations between patrons and clients occur not through daily arm-twisting, but through the advent and survival of governments whose values and policies are compatible with those of the patron. Whatever their critics may claim, such regimes are not necessarily installed by electoral fraud, on the bayonets of US marines or at the behest of the CIA. The regimes reflect a need to be acceptable to outsiders, a need that applies to all governments but happens to be particularly intense, exclusive, and persuasive in the case of countries heavily influenced over a long period by one powerful outsider.

Indeed, with countries as pervasively influenced as Cuba and the Philippines, the very term *outsider* is virtually obsolete. Such societies live, in their government and in individual lives, a deep and permanent inner battle between instincts to embrace and to reject the United States, the expression of either being natural and creating its own logic. Neither pro-Americanism (as the left suspects) nor anti-Americanism (as the right assumes) needs external encouragement to take political form: By this point, both are mental habits. Such habits can be found in the equally ambivalent relationships between former colonial powers and their ex-dependents.

This said, it does matter which reflex prevails. Contrary to the prejudices of many dependency theorists, clients do break out. The anti-American camp may prevail: Once installed, it will benefit from the legitimacy and material forms of power that sustained its predecessor and will be as well protected against outside interference by international norms against intervention. Indeed, its domestic and foreign enemies may also be deterred by the prospect of having to deal with a powerful patron, the difference being that the patron in question may now have one or more red stars on its flag rather than fifty white ones.

REGIMES IN CRISIS: PATTERNS AND PATHOLOGY

All this suggests that the impending collapse of a client is, both for diplomats and scholars, a crisis that will almost certainly illuminate and may well jeopardize vital investments and commitments. The crisis may not, of course, pass beyond the point of impending collapse: Aid may be sent, domestic support may rally, and the regime may survive.

Some clients, indeed, may deliberately encourage premature reports of their demise so as to attract the attention and support of a patron whom they suspect of furtive or imminent faithlessness. Several observers suspected that the "crises" in Zaire in the late 1970s were at least in part a case of self-induced swooning on the part of President Mobutu--a form of blackmail intended to coerce American and Western European governments into defending the indefensible for fear of something even nastier taking its place. If so, the tactic worked admirably.

Another tactic is to attract support, not by exaggerating or inventing a threat so much as by circulating dark allegations about its real source (as with Somoza's allegations about Communist influence within the US government). South African governments, like European colonial governments, have consistently tried to diminish foreign sympathy for African nationalists by claiming that apparently innocuous demands for equality and democracy are actually vehicles for organizations dedicated to spreading communism.

When a crisis actually runs its course to the point that a regime falls and a vacuum appears to develop, it will run through a sequence observable in other cases. This sequence involves fairly distinct phases, each with its own characteristic dilemmas, realignments, and redefinitions. As the crisis deepens, the range of choices open to patrons and clients will narrow in an ominously similar fashion.

Again, in looking at the phases and patterns of crisis, it is vital to look behind the surface diplomatic and political activity to the equally striking cognitive and rhetorical changes that occur and that also show certain patterns. The dilemmas faced by politicians and officials turn out to be similar when we compare cases: so, too, do the reactions and the redefinitions that occur as a "legitimacy crisis" deepens to become a succession crisis.

Just as we find common patterns in the choices and strategies open to governments, whether in the country concerned or abroad, we find common patterns of perception and definition. Cycles of crisis are accompanied by characteristic psychological and political sequences--reactions of denial, changing "definitions of the situation" and attributions of responsibility, as well as political realignments--that accompany the diplomatic moves with which we are mainly concerned.

Without prejudging analysis of the cases that follow, it may be helpful to suggest a framework for comparing succession crises. This framework refers to the phases that commonly occur in such crises.

1. The Status Quo

This "phase" really comprises the entire history preceding the emergence of a serious challenge to the regime. The central issue here is the range of interests, investments, and commitments that have shaped and sustained the status quo coalition--those American and foreign politicians and officials who are committed to the established patron-client relationship and the interests it protects. In examining and comparing the cases, we need to understand the history and recent character of the relationship between the foreign regime and the United States. Specifically, we might ask:

   a.   *How long had the relationship endured?*
   b.   *What range of interests was involved in this relationship?*
   c.   *How had the relationship been justified and defended?*
   d.   *What were the domestic sources of support for the relationship (both in the United States and in the country concerned)?*
   e.   *Through what channels did such support express itself?*
   f.   *How personalized had the relationship become?*

2. The Regime Under Attack

As a domestic challenge to the regime emerges and grows, we can often identify two phases, distinguished by the responses of both the client regime and its foreign patron.

The first phase we can term *reinforcement*. This response involves denial or minimization of the threat and a belief on the part of central figures in the status quo coalition that, with suitable measures of accommodation or repression, any danger can be averted. The regime is, in the eyes of its foreign supporters, salvageable. In the eyes of its leaders and its domestic supporters, it is clearly legitimate and deserves words and acts of encouragement from foreign allies.

The second phase involves, at least for the patron, reassessment. This process is likely to begin among those less personally involved in the forging and maintenance of the relationship in question. It entails the uprooting of assumptions that have lain undisturbed and the levering apart of some distinctions that have become glued together.

Reassessment works at different levels but becomes more fundamental as the crisis deepens. Participants and observers start to challenge assumptions about the legitimacy and power of the client regime; those concerned about the patron's stake abroad begin to question the identification of (in this case) American national interest with the continuation of the regime. Policymakers start worrying about the reliability of intelligence and about its interpretation. In effect, an intellectual separation appears, foreshadowing a possible political separation.

Such a process may in fact occur on both sides. The client regime quietly begins looking around for an alternative patron in case it is abandoned by its supposedly loyal ally. Equally quietly, the patron is likely to start sending out feelers to possible successors to the incumbent regime.

3. Negotiating the Succession

Three further phases may now follow, which we might call *delegitimation*, *realignment*, and *relegitimation*. By this stage in the crisis, the entire relation ship, its rationale, and a wide range of alternatives are up on the hoist for scrutiny by the various interested--and increasingly agitated--parties. Severe political battles are likely to break out within policymaking circles on both sides, and intermediaries, such as ambassadors, may find their loyalties and judgments called into question. Often, some people actually lose their jobs at this stage, possibly because the orthodox wisdom with which they are associated is beginning to crumble, but sometimes simply because their superiors have decided to break from established policy; new appointments are a well-understood symbol of such change.

As the crisis reaches a climax, it will engage ever-higher levels of official-dom, until the chief executive is actively and frequently involved. As this occurs, the formal system of diplomatic communication is likely to be duplicated or even superseded by more direct and secret communication between heads of state, often through trusted personal intermediaries (such as Senator Paul Laxalt in the Philippines crisis). Paradoxically, such direct communication is likely to expand just as actual and would-be policymakers have developed a consensus that the client regime is doomed.

As the crisis moves into the phases of realignment and relegitimation, both sides strive to hold onto the belief that they have some control over events. Though comforting, this belief may well be illusory. On the patron's side, it often takes the form of believing that acquiescing in and expediting the removal of the incumbent will earn credit with those set on taking over from the collapsing regime. Such credit can be used, it is thought, to influence the succession (specifically, the selection of members of the next government and the latter's decisions on basic issues of foreign and domestic policy).

At this point, such a belief is likely to be deluded. Since the defining feature of the crisis is general rejection of the regime, such rejection is likely to extend to its patron. Until it has firmly established its own authority, the domestic opposition needs to be seen as heading the forces of rejection. Its authority depends on its keeping a reputation for obduracy, and especially obduracy toward any outsiders blamed for encouraging or prolonging the outgoing regime's tyranny. So, far from sharing credit with (in this case) the United States for removing the regime, the opposition needs to show that it alone was responsible for the removal, or at least that it led the revolution.

The outcome and aftermath of the succession struggle will illuminate the question of what kinds of interests--strategic, economic, or otherwise--the patron has in the foreign country concerned. If policymakers believe that such interests are permanent and substantial, they will feel bound to try to create a relationship with the new regime that at least insures these interests. In this process, a degree of relegitimation inevitably occurs.

This effort to create a new relationship necessarily involves a continuation of the debates around fundamental issues set off by the crisis of the fallen regime. How far are American interests compatible with the sort ofcommit-ment that is likely to develop with recognition of the regime? What will the new regime want as its price for defending American interests? Is this price one that may draw the United States into another uncomfortably close relationship with a regime whose domestic authority may soon decay and become yet another Tar Baby?

ANALYTIC ISSUES

The cases in this volume lend themselves to discussion of several important issues in the analysis of international relations. Three such issues are considered below: the analysis of international negotiation, foreign policy evaluation, and "bureaucratic politics."

International Negotiation

Negotiation may play a large, a small, or no role in the development and resolution of the kinds of crises depicted in this volume. There is nothing in the character of such crises that makes them especially suitable for resolution by negotiation rather than by armed intervention or popular insurrection. (Nor are they really susceptible to "management," despite the use of this word in some American official discussion--the only "managing" usually discernible is that synonymous with coping and survival.[4])

Yet negotiation, if not management, often does take place, and it is easy to see why. Conventionally (and correctly), negotiation is said to be appropriate when the parties concerned have interests in common, when none can impose its preferences on the others, and when each has a veto. This combination of circumstances can arise at any stage in a succession crisis, and most commonly involves US government representatives and the failing leader and/or his presumptive heirs (whether collective or competing). At an early stage, it may be concerned with finding discreet ways to reestablish the authority of the leader; later, it may be concerned with detaching and co-opting elements of the opposition (as in the Nicaraguan mediation in late 1978) or with bringing about a gracious departure for a doomed head of state.

But such negotiation does not always occur. Even if it does, it may be marginal or, indeed, incidental to the outcome of the main struggle, which is decided by force of arms, abdication, or organized political pressure. Nevertheless, significant negotiations may occur, between (for example) the outgoing leader or his supporters and aspiring successors, or between US officials and leaders of the opposition. Negotiations may also occur on the US side, notably between officials and members of Congress.

Foreign Policy Evaluation

As suggested above, succession crises typically raise fundamental questions about the rationale, costs, and benefits of American relations with a country. They require policymakers (and leaders of public opinion) to think in a radical fashion about the relationship between interests and commitments that supposedly guides foreign policy.

The cases examined here therefore provide an excellent context for starting discussions about basic problems:

1. *The problem of determining goals, assessing their feasibility and their compatibility with each other, and deciding upon appropriate strategies.* In crises of the kind depicted in this volume, it is essential to be clear about what American goals are relative to the situation as it changes and about what values underpin these goals. It is also important to be able to discern and assess realistically what can be done to reach such goals, to be able to measure the probable costs and benefits of different courses of action, and to decide which to try, which to keep in reserve, and which to forget.

2. *The problem of interpreting and weighing evidence.* "Strategizing" depends on an agreed and relatively stable "definition of the situation." To know what is happening and to know what it means in what is, by definition, a fluid and usually confused political crisis is both vital and usually very difficult. The four cases in this book provide some dramatic examples of the problem of "perception" and "cognition" so widely mentioned in writing on international affairs. They also, however, demonstrate what is less generally acknowledged in such writing--the intrinsic difficulty of establishing a dependable interpretation of essentially ambiguous, often seemingly contradictory events and behavior.

3. *The problem of evaluating performance.* Succession crises provide salutary evidence for the observation that the adoption of a "strategy" does not necessarily mean that anything happens as a result or that all the parts of the vaunted strategy are understood or implemented as the strategists intend. Failure or underperformance may be due to poor communication, insufficient thought about who is to do or say what, active opposition (whether from the junior ranks in the hierarchy or from others hostile to the policy adopted), individual frailties or preoccupations, or plain bad luck. The cases offer many opportunities to discuss why apparently elegant and logical strategies fail. They also illustrate some fundamental conceptual problems in any policy evaluation, namely:

    a.   *how to determine what is "success" and what is "failure";*
    b.   *how to decide what is sufficiently conclusive evidence of either;*
    c.   *how to determine when such evidence is sufficiently available; and*
    d.   *how to make a summary but reliable conclusion about what caused success or failure so as to be able to decide what to try next.*

"Bureaucratic Politics"

A common feature of crises of the kind depicted in the volume is that they set off related crises in governments elsewhere, principally here in the government of the United States. Although in periods of stability a minor fire in the Washington policymaking edifice is likely to cause a large conflagration (or at least fear of one) in the capitals governed by client regimes, in periods of crisis for the latter a reverse chain of ignition is likely to occur. Disagreement and conflict are apt to break out in Washington: Having broken out, they are apt to become public and to some extent observable as the warring parties go in search of allies and sympathy. Would-be political firefighters, insurers, realtors, and plain voyeurs (not to mention arsonists) can learn much from observing how the fire spreads, who is good at putting it out, who escapes, what exits successful escapees use (and when), who gets left behind, and who ends up cleaning up the mess, paying the bills, and burying the dead.

Each of the four case chapters contains questions and exercises relating to these issues; the narrative halts at suitable points for class discussions and simulations. The chapters themselves are, with one exception, compounds of cases originally written separately for the Pew Initiative in Diplomatic Training. The exception is the first case study--with slight changes and some editing, it reproduces a case by Pamela K. Starr and Abraham F. Lowenthal entitled *The United States and the Cuban Revolution: 1958-1960* (Pew case no. 328). The other three are derived as follows from Pew cases:

1. "Nicaragua, 1978-1979" is based on Douglas A. Chalmers, *Nicaragua, 1978-1979: The United States and Anastasio Somoza. Dealing with Friendly Dictators Who Are Losing Their Authority* (Pew case no. 105); Alex Roberto Hybel, *The United States and Nicaragua: Anatomy of a Failed Negotiation for Regime Change, 1977-1979* (Pew case no. 327); and Rachel McCleary, *The Ethics of Intervention: The United States and Nicaragua* (Pew case no. 347).

2. "Iran, 1978-1979" is based on Gregory F. Treverton with James Klocke, *The Fall of the Shah of Iran* (Pew case no. 311) and Andrew Steigman, *The Iranian Hostage Negotiations, November 1979-January 1981* (Pew case no. 348).

3. "The Philippines, 1985-1986" is based on William E. Kline, *The Fall of Marcos* (Pew case no. 439) and Donald M. Goldstein, *US Policy Concerning Renewal of the Military Base Agreement with the Philippines* (Pew case no. 325). Two other Pew cases were consulted in preparing the chapter--Douglas J. Macdonald, *"To Save the Philippine Republic": The Decision to Reform the Government of the Philippines, 1949-1951* (Pew case no. 440) and Penelope Walker, *Political Crisis and Debt Negotiations: The Case of the Philippines, 1983-1986* (Pew case no. 133).

In each of these three chapters, the material in the original cases has been supplemented by material from commercially published sources. These and other secondary sources are listed under "Further Reading" at the end of each chapter.

NOTES

1. Mauricio Solaun, ex-US ambassador to Nicaragua, quoted in Bernard Diederich, *Somoza and the Legacy of U.S. Involvement in Central America* (New York: E. P. Dutton, 1981), 144-145.

2. Bruce E. Moon, "Consensus or Compliance? Foreign-policy Change and External Dependence," *International Organization* 39, 2 (Spring 1985), 297-329.

3. The term *dependency theory* refers to a body of writing (principally by Latin American scholars such as Fernando Cardoso, Theotonio dos Santos, and Osvaldo Sunkel, but also by others such as Andre Gunder Frank and Peter Evans) that presents developing countries as the historical objects of a dependence-creating process that permeates domestic economic and political structures. The central dynamics of the process are typically identified as economic, the "political" and "cultural" being assumed to be derivative from and expressive of economic dependence.

4. It may be comforting to feel that such management, usually through negotiators, is feasible. Admittedly, subsequent reconstructions, especially by policymakers involved, often give an impression that a particular crisis was actually "managed" and always under control. Examine the finer details, however, and compare accounts, and a less blandly reassuring picture appears--that of a small boat tossed on a stormy sea.

2

CUBA, 1958–1959
The Fall of Fulgencio Batista

The first case in the book describes the events leading up to the overthrow in January 1959 of the Cuban dictator Fulgencio Batista by guerrilla forces under the leadership of Fidel Castro. This episode involved the first serious challenge to an established US client by a movement with Marxist (and possibly Soviet) associations within the Western hemisphere. Occurring at a delicate point in the Cold War, it presented US policymakers with all the major dilemmas characteristic of regime crises and did so in an especially acute and immediate fashion since the country concerned lay less than 100 miles from the coast of Florida. The case exemplifies both the procedural problems created for a patron government by such crises and the conflict of values commonly besetting US administrations when they occur--essentially, a conflict between the wish to protect what are seen as vital diplomatic and geopolitical interests and the wish to avoid charges of interference and "imperialism."

*　　*　　*

In April 1958, the 26th of July Movement--the anti-Batista rebels led by Fidel Castro--called a general strike in support of its military offensive against the Cuban government of Fulgencio Batista, but the strike fizzled. This failure convinced the Batista regime that the rebels were now vulnerable to a government offensive. By August, however, this "final offensive" against the rebels

---

This chapter is an edited version of the case study by Pamela K. Starr and Abraham F. Lowenthal, The United States and the Cuban Revolution: 1958-1960, *Pew case study no. 328.*

had ended in a decisive defeat for the government forces. The rebel victory, demonstrating that the Batista government might be too weak to survive much longer, transformed Fidel Castro into a symbol of national resistance to the Batista regime. Within a few months, the US government was facing the imminent collapse of that regime.

THE STATUS QUO

Cuba achieved its independence from Spain in 1898 in a war that Americans call the Spanish-American War but that Cubans refer to as their War of Independence. During the fighting, threats to the limited US business interests in Cuba and exaggerated US press reports of alleged Spanish cruelty against the Cuban revolutionaries created a strong pro-interventionist sentiment in the United States. In this environment, Spanish refusal to meet the US demand for Cuban independence prompted the United States to declare war against Spain in April 1898. The peace treaty ending this short confrontation provided for nominal Cuban political independence under US military occupation.

As a condition for the withdrawal of US forces, the United States forced the drafters of the Cuban Constitution to include the Platt Amendment, which greatly limited the sovereignty of the new Cuban nation. The amendment granted the United States the right to oversee Cuban international commitments and government finances, establish a naval base at Guantanamo Bay, and intervene to preserve Cuban independence or maintain political stability and "adequate" government. Following the end of the military occupation in 1902, the United States further ensured its high-profile role in Cuban affairs by incorporating the provisions of the Platt Amendment in a bilateral treaty. A Reciprocal Trade Agreement between the two nations also enhanced US economic influence in Cuba; it established incentives for increased bilateral trade and investment. Cuba thus began its independent history as a virtual protectorate of the United States.

Repeated overt intervention in Cuban affairs marked the pursuit of Washington's three Cuban policy objectives during the first two decades of US-Cuban relations. The United States responded to a 1905 electoral dispute by reoccupying Cuba for three years (1906-1909); an American actually served as the president of Cuba during this time. Political disturbances in 1912 and 1917 also led to the landing of US troops to reestablish order. And in response to disputed elections and threatened instability again in 1921,

President Warren Harding sent an adviser to Cuba to supervise the peaceful resolution of political disputes and encourage political and economic reforms. In carrying out these directives, however, the "adviser" acted as a virtual proconsul; he effectively divested the Cuban president of his decisionmaking powers, personally appointed a new cabinet, and undertook budget reforms.

Such frequent and forceful intervention in Cuban affairs was accompanied by a rapid expansion of American involvement in the Cuban economy. By the end of World War I, the United States had replaced Europe as the dominant foreign economic presence in Cuba. By the 1920s, total US investment in Cuba was over $1 billion; US companies controlled the electricity and telephone industries, invested extensively in railroads and banking, and owned port facilities, manufacturing firms, over 60 percent of the sugar industry, and over 20 percent of all Cuban territory. This expansive US economic presence exacerbated Cuba's economic vulnerability and increased its dependence on the United States. Large-scale US investment in the Cuban sugar industry helped to accentuate Cuba's existing tendencies toward a sugar-based monoculture economy with its boom and bust economic cycles tied to the rise and decline of the world sugar price. At the same time, the Reciprocal Trade Agreement increased Cuban dependence on sugar exports to the United States (in the 1920s, Cuba exported 95 percent of its sugar crop to the United States). This dependence undermined the ability of the Cuban government to mitigate the negative impact of these economic fluctuations because Cuban access to the US market was determined unilaterally by the US government, independent of Cuban economic needs. The Cuban government, therefore, was unable to increase its sugar exports to compensate for revenue lost due to falling international sugar prices.

Cuba's substantial economic and political dependence on the United States deeply influenced Cuban politics. During Cuba's first two independent decades, the Cuban elite chose not to fight North American tutelage but rather to exploit it for personal benefit, even at the expense of national interests. The 1906 US reoccupation of Cuba and the 1917 intervention were in response to the Cuban president's request for assistance, ostensibly to restore order but actually to prevent political rivals from occupying the presidency. The interventions of 1912 and 1921, although unsolicited, were not energetically opposed either. Further, since the elite generally benefited from the US economic presence in Cuba, it did not attempt to limit its growth.

The Cuban elite's essentially antinationalist attitude toward US intervention in Cuban domestic affairs engendered two further political developments-- the discrediting of the traditional Cuban political elite and the rise of anti-American nationalism. The interplay among these mutually reinforcing tendencies strongly influenced the course of Cuban politics and developments in US-Cuban relations from 1898 until Fidel Castro took power in 1959.

In response to continuing instability and the rise of anti-American sentiment in Cuba, the United States began to adopt more subtle policy mechanisms--actions designed to advance US interests in Cuba while limiting direct US involvement in Cuban domestic affairs. The first sign of this policy realignment was President Harding's 1921 nonmilitary response to Cuban political instability, followed by reduced direct US control over Cuban domestic affairs. The government of Gerardo Machado (elected to the Cuban presidency in 1925) reinforced this policy shift by willingly protecting US economic and security interests in Cuba. By the time of the next political crisis, the 1929 uprisings in opposition to Machado, a new US policy toward Cuba was evident--the United States would permit substantial Cuban freedom of action in domestic matters as long as US interests in Cuba were not directly threatened.

Political instability returned to Cuba in the wake of President Machado's fraudulent reelection and the onset of the Great Depression. In line with its new policy approach, the United States initially did not intervene in Cuban affairs. But in 1933, radical, nationalistic elements of the opposition, perceived by decisionmakers in Washington to threaten US interests, appeared on the verge of victory. The US ambassador actively intervened to stop these groups taking power, but his efforts were unsuccessful. In September 1933 the nationalist opposition came into power under the leadership of Ramon Grau San Martin.

Although US decisionmakers were not in complete agreement about how the United States should respond to the Grau government, they shared the belief that the new regime included radical, potentially Communist elements, threatened US economic interests, and probably could not restore stability in Cuba. Unwilling to intervene militarily, the Roosevelt administration withheld diplomatic recognition, cultivated anti-Grau opposition forces in Cuba, and stationed US warships off the Cuban coast. Within four months, a military coup led by Fulgencio Batista, who had been courted by the US ambassador, ousted Grau's nationalist regime.

These events reinforced the Cuban sense of "geographic fatalism" and suggested to many Cubans that the United States simply would not permit any meaningful reduction of Cuban dependence on its northern neighbor. The outcome of the 1933 revolution also had long-term repercussions for the Cuban political system. By the end of the 1930s, the new Cuban political elite, including most of the leaders of the 1933 revolution, had accepted the limitations on their freedom of political action imposed by Cuban dependence on the United States. This passivity in the face of US hegemony increasingly appeared as antinationalist as previous Cuban government behavior and gradually undermined government legitimacy once again. Further, while the events of 1933 temporarily quieted overt expressions of radical Cuban nationalism, this episode also deepened the latent nationalist and anti-American sentiments of the Cuban people.

The 1933 revolution also led to further changes in US policy toward Cuba. Washington moved further away from direct meddling in the island's internal affairs and toward a policy designed to establish a bilateral environment that would enable Cuban governments to maintain internal order and protect US interests. After eliminating the immediate threat to US interests in Cuba, the Roosevelt administration shifted its attention to the potential long-term threat posed by anti-American nationalism and continuing instability. To accommodate Cuban nationalist concerns, the administration abrogated the Platt Amendment. To reinforce economic and political stability, it negotiated a new Reciprocal Trade Agreement with Cuba. The new agreement maintained incentives to bilateral economic ties and, more important, regularized Cuban access to the US sugar market through a system of annual quotas. US decisionmakers seemed to believe that these policy changes would reduce anti-American sentiment, reinforce the positive effects of the close US-Cuban relationship, and prevent new anti-American governments from coming to power.

These revisions in US policy, together with Cuba's political stability under a succession of governments controlled by Batista (1934-1944) and then the opposition Autentico party (1944-1952), combined to reduce frictions in US-Cuban relations for over two decades. The United States briefly focused on Cuban affairs following a further coup by Batista in 1952, but after concluding that the new regime would not undermine US interests, Washington extended diplomatic recognition and turned its attention elsewhere.

The Cuban public, however, did not accept Batista's coup as readily as the United States. Although the deposed regime had been marked by corruption, inefficiency, and violence, it had been based on constitutional norms and established political expectations. Batista's coup, followed by his fraudulent election to the presidency in 1954, destroyed the constitutional legitimacy of government. Opposition to Batista developed rapidly, and long-frustrated Cuban nationalism reemerged.

Batista's cultivation of very close ties with the United States further inflamed Cuban nationalism while also rekindling anti-Americanism. Batista aligned Cuba closely with US foreign policy, outlawed the Cuban Communist party, established an extremely close friendship with the US ambassador, and ensured a favorable climate for US investments in Cuba. In return for such friendly behavior, the Batista regime received increased US economic and military assistance as well as US political support.

The regime's generous incentives for foreign investment also led to a renewed expansion of the US economic presence in Cuba. Although American involvement in the sugar industry had declined to about one-third of Cuban sugar production by 1958 (from its 1929 high of 62.5 percent), US interests continued to dominate the public utilities sector, substantially broadened their prominent position in banking and manufacturing, and expanded rapidly into petroleum and tourism--particularly in hotels and casinos. All told, US direct private investment in Cuba increased over 46 percent between 1953 and 1958 to a total book value of over $1 billion.

Batista's policies thus helped create an intimate relationship with the United States; a relationship so close that Americans sometimes referred to Cuba as the "49th state." But this close relationship also visibly exposed Cuban dependence on the United States, offended Cuban nationalist sentiments, and closely associated the United States with the perpetuation of an increasingly discredited and detested regime.

The International Context:
US Interests and Objectives

US policy toward Cuba prior to 1958 rested on three principal, interrelated objectives. The central aim was exclude the influence of other foreign powers by expanding US influence. Because Cuba is located only 90 miles from the US coast and sits astride major sea lanes into the Caribbean, the United States long considered Cuba to be of great geostrategic importance. The completion of the Panama Canal in 1914 had made it especially important for the United States to prevent foreign influence over Cuba and had given Washington more power to achieve this objective.

The specific targets encompassed by the American policy of excluding external influence varied over time; they changed in response to shifting international power relationships. At the turn of the century, when Western European influence in Cuba was still fairly strong, the United States aimed to expand its influence in Cuba primarily at Western European expense. After the United States became the dominant foreign influence in Cuba by the end of World War I, US policy successfully prevented renewed European involvement in Cuba. The expansion of German international power and influence during the late 1930s and early 1940s shifted the focus of US policy again;

Washington aimed to hinder German activity in Cuba and the Caribbean. With the advent of the Cold War, the United States turned its attention to barring the introduction of Soviet influence into Cuba.

A second, closely related objective was to maintain general hemispheric stability. The United States had long believed that political and economic instability would provide opportunities for foreign intervention in the Americas. The American goal of excluding foreign power influence from Cuba, therefore, required political and economic stability in Cuba. The Platt Amendment, until it was abrogated in 1934, gave the United States a legal right to ensure such stability. In ensuing years, Washington relied on friendly Cuban governments to maintain order on the island. The United States also sought to protect and expand US trade and investment in Cuba, not only to enhance US influence but also to bolster Cuban political and economic stability.

The third continuing US objective in Cuba was to prevent the establishment of a radical, anti-American regime. Throughout this century, US decisionmakers have argued that such a regime would seriously threaten US interests in Cuba, partly due to the instability commonly accompanying and following the rise of radical regimes. More importantly, a radical, anti-American government in Cuba would try to expand Cuban independence from the United States by reducing US influence in Cuban affairs; it might modify established trade and investment policies, nationalize US properties, and even establish an alliance with a US adversary. In short, a radical regime in Cuba would threaten US interests in Cuba by undermining the preceding two US policy objectives.

US policy toward Cuba was also affected by more general geopolitical considerations, especially the changing international behavior of the Soviet Union in the late 1950s. In the early years of the Cold War, the Soviet Union had limited its international involvement to its border regions. But by the late 1950s, under the leadership of Nikita Khrushchev, Soviet foreign policy exhibited a new activism designed to displace US international influence, particularly in the underdeveloped countries, and to establish the Soviet Union as a world power. The Soviets had also shown that they were able to project their influence beyond Eastern Europe; this was most visibly demonstrated by the October 1957 launch of Sputnik, the first man-made satellite to orbit the Earth.

International developments emanating from these changes in Soviet foreign policy created substantial concern in Washington. The Soviets expanded their involvement in the Middle East, thereby contributing to President Eisenhower's July 1958 decision to land marines in Lebanon. Even more unsettling to the United States, in November 1958 Khrushchev threatened to expel Great Britain, France, and the United States from Berlin. Within this tense environment, however, the Soviet Union also betrayed a desire to reduce tensions between the superpowers by proposing a policy of "peaceful coexistence" with the United States; the Soviets agreed to discuss a long-standing US proposal to ban nuclear weapons tests and suggested creating a nuclear-free zone in Central Europe, arms reductions in Germany, and a nonaggression treaty between the superpowers. In other words, the Soviets seemed ready either to increase conflict or to cooperate more closely with the United States. The ambiguous and urgent character of Soviet actions during this period demanded much of US decisionmakers' attention and thus reduced the time available to consider other foreign policy developments.

Circumstances in Latin America also influenced the US response to Batista's decline. In 1936, the United States had signed a regional nonintervention pact that prohibited outside interference in the internal affairs of hemispheric states. Postwar US decisionmakers, seeing this agreement as an essential element of Inter-American Cold War cooperation, expanded and reinforced the regional commitment to nonintervention in two postwar treaties: the Rio Treaty and the Charter of the Organization of American States (OAS). An interventionist US response to Cuban developments, therefore, would not simply elicit Latin American opposition to US actions; it could also undermine the hemisphere's united front against Soviet aggression. Further, the widespread Latin American opposition to the Batista regime, including material support for the Castro-led revolutionaries from several Latin American governments, ensured that any US action in support of Batista would have negative repercussions for US-Latin American relations.

Domestic Politics and US Policy

The lingering effects of McCarthyism had a significant impact on the perceptions and policy recommendations of US decisionmakers in the late 1950s. The 1949 Communist victory in China convinced many members of Congress, including Republican Senator Joseph McCarthy (R-WI), that US foreign policy was being undermined by the infiltration of Communists and Communist sympathizers into the federal bureaucracy. These accusations incited a massive search for Communists, particularly in the State Department, perceived to be most responsible for the "loss of China." The ensuing purges made State Department survivors hesitant to oppose antiCommunist dictators and/or to support reformist opposition movements in underdeveloped countries. Although the impact of McCarthyism had faded somewhat by the late 1950s, particularly among recently hired personnel, it still engendered a cautious approach toward instability in the underdeveloped countries among high-level State Department officials.

The attitude of US news media, as a molder as well as a reflector of US public opinion, also affected the domestic environment within which Washington responded to Cuban developments. Despite general disregard for Latin American events during the 1950s, the media focused critical attention on US support for the repressive Batista government. A series of articles in the *New York Times* also painted a favorable picture of the Castro-led rebels as democratic reformers who only resorted to violence as a last resort. But the broader media portrayal of the Cuban rebels was much more reserved, while concern with the situation in Cuba remained moderate.

THE REGIME UNDER ATTACK

The Character of the Opposition

As opposition to Batista mounted during the 1950s, the regime resorted to ever-heavier repression. Yet the character of the opposition--specifically, the 26th of July Movement--and its leader was hazy as far as US decision-makers were concerned.

The movement had articulated anti-American sentiments in some of its statements and actions. In June and July of 1958, it kidnapped US citizens and cut off water supply to the US naval base at Guantanamo Bay; some of its proposed reforms threatened the interests of American property owners in Cuba. Equally disconcerting to the United States, two of Fidel Castro's closest associates, his brother Raul and Ernesto "Che" Guevarra, appeared to embrace elements of Marxist ideology, and two other high-level officials had been closely associated with members of Cuba's Communist party, the Popular Socialist party (PSP).

Yet PSP members were notably absent from the movement's leadership, and with only a few exceptions, the rebels had excluded PSP members from their ranks. The 26th of July Movement also counted many moderates as members, enjoyed increasing Cuban middle-class support, and had presented a moderate, albeit skeletal, political program. In addition, the rebels had attempted to cultivate American goodwill before and after the events of June and July 1958. Finally, the movement had agreed to a power-sharing arrangement with less radical Cuban opposition forces to form a unified Cuban opposition movement, the Civic Revolutionary Front. Fidel Castro was chosen to lead the Front's military forces, but he in turn designated a political moderate, Manuel Urrutia Lleo, as the future provisional president of any post-Batista government led by the Civic Revolutionary Front.

Fidel Castro's character appeared equally ambiguous. He supported policies that US decisionmakers believed were associated often with Communists, including agrarian reform and regulation of public utilities. But intelligence reports offered no evidence that Castro favored establishing communism in Cuba. He sharply criticized the United States for intervention in Latin American affairs while professing to harbor no animosity toward the United States. He spoke of restoring democratic government in Cuba, but his inexperience in government and his apparently unquenchable thirst for power led US intelligence to conclude that democracy might not follow a Civic Revolutionary Front provisional government.

US Responses to the Crisis

By 1957, the regime's growing unpopularity in Cuba, and particularly its use of repression, raised questions in Washington about the continuing ability of the Batista government to protect US interests in Cuba. In an unsuccessful attempt to pressure Batista to reform his policies, the State Department replaced its ambassador to Cuba with a new appointee not personally identified with the dictator, Earl E.T. Smith. Batista's refusal to respond to this pressure, combined with his illegal use of US-supplied weapons in his fight against rebel uprisings, led to a stronger expression of US displeasure with his regime--the suspension of arms shipments in March 1958.

This action, unintentionally, helped to hasten the deterioration of Batista's political position. Cubans believed the suspension of arms shipments indicated a withdrawal of US support for Batista; according to the lessons of Cuban history, this was thought to spell the end of his regime. As a result, Batista's remaining supporters increasingly abandoned the government.

In mid-1958, the Cuban army mounted its unsuccessful offensive against the rebel movement led by Fidel Castro. For the first time, Washington began to wonder whether the Batista government would survive. Concerned about Batista's refusal to undertake reforms while his grip on power was waning, the United States began to consider alternative ways to protect its interests in Cuba.

DISCUSSION QUESTIONS

1. *What options did the United States have at this point?*
2. *Did the United States have enough information to be able to weigh these options properly?*
3. *To what extent were US interests and objectives threatened at this point in the crisis?*

NEGOTIATING THE SUCCESSION?

Throughout the autumn of 1958, Batista's position continued to deteriorate. The November 3, 1958, presidential election, held under pressure from the United States, did not help shore up the regime's popular support as the United States had hoped. To the contrary, the clearly fraudulent election of Batista's handpicked successor further intensified public opposition.

By the end of November, fully 80 percent of the Cuban public opposed the regime and were considered unlikely to support Batista's "elected" successor, Andres Rivero Aguero. The regime's survival was now completely dependent on the continued support of the Cuban armed forces. Batista, however, refused to resign in favor of a provisional government controlled by his opponents. Instead, he declared a state of emergency and maintained the suspension of constitutional guarantees.

US Assessments and Strategies

The US response to the apparent weakening of the Batista government reflected policymakers' shared conceptions of the constellation of events surrounding the Cuban case. Foremost among these was their understanding of the nature of Soviet foreign policy. They saw a Communist adversary continually trying to expand its international influence by undermining democratic, capitalist, and pro-United States regimes throughout the world. The Soviets' preferred technique, it was thought, was to exploit instability, particularly in the underdeveloped countries, by spreading the Communist ideology and anti-Americanism through their surrogates, national Communist parties. Consequently, the United States had to be prepared constantly to counter such Soviet threats.

By the end of 1958, US decisionmakers also increasingly agreed that the US containment policy should be modified to include government-financed development assistance and support for economic and political reforms. Such policies were designed to alleviate the conditions that created opportunities for Communist meddling.

A second shared conception was the need to refrain from intervention in the internal affairs of Latin American states in order to maintain amicable hemispheric relations. Communist involvement, however, was thought to imply a Soviet attempt to undermine US interests in Latin America and thus to transform a strictly internal matter into an international affair. In this situation, decisionmakers agreed that the United States should not be limited by its nonintervention pledge; but decisionmakers did not agree on what constituted non-intervention or what demonstrated Communist meddling in Latin American politics.

US government officials also generally agreed that the Batista regime was no longer able to provide adequate protection for American interests in Cuba and that the regime could not survive without US assistance. Further, unless the United States successfully supported a third-force government, Fidel Castro was thought to be the most likely successor to Batista. Decisionmakers did not agree, however, on the best way to achieve this outcome.

Despite Batista's tenuous hold on power and the increasing power and popularity of the rebel opposition, it still appeared to US officials that the regime would last at least another two months, during which the United States might be able to engineer a peaceful transition of power advantageous to US interests. But serious differences of opinion about the crisis and about ways of dealing with it surfaced in Washington. These differences were expressed in arguments between (and even within) agencies.

Within the State Department, most of the staff working in Washington (including the two highest-ranking officials concerned with the Cuban situation, Assistant Secretary of State for Latin American Affairs R. Richard Rubottom and Director of Caribbean Affairs William Wieland) felt the available evidence did not demonstrate that the 26th of July Movement was Communist-dominated or that Castro was a Communist sympathizer. (A majority of those serving in the US Embassy in Havana also took this view.) However, the majority at State did not trust Castro and generally agreed that a Castro-led government would not be in the best interests of the United States.

On the question of US action, the officials concerned felt that any attempt to prop up Batista's unpopular regime would only prolong Cuban instability while provoking widespread Latin American criticism of US intervention in Cuba's internal affairs. Further, they argued that since the problem remained an internal Cuban matter, a lasting solution could be developed best by the Cubans with only limited US guidance. In addition, the presence of a number of anti-Castro opposition groups capable of establishing a popular government suggested the possibility of a third-force solution acceptable to the United States.

The majority of department personnel proposed that the United States maintain its nonintervention policy by keeping up the arms embargo against the Batista government, continuing to refuse support for Castro's rebels, and closely monitoring Cuban development for indications of Communist involvement. But these officials also perceived a need for US action to promote a gradual and orderly transition of power by pressuring Batista to step down and providing limited, behind-the-scenes support for anti-Castro opposition groups capable of establishing a provisional government following Batista's resignation. The potential contradiction between these two policy proposals, however, resulted in half-hearted pursuit of a provisional government; even this limited American involvement bordered on intervention in Cuban internal affairs.

A very small but vocal group within the State Department, including the new US ambassador to Cuba, Earl E.T. Smith, strongly disagreed with the majority position. These officials were convinced that the available evidence sufficiently demonstrated that the 26th of July Movement was Communist-dominated, that Castro was a Communist sympathizer, and that a rebel government would inevitably threaten US interests in Cuba. Despite its flaws, therefore, the Batista regime had to be preserved. Recognizing that Batista personally probably could not remain in power, this minority insisted that the regime could be, and must be, sustained under the leadership of President-elect Rivero Aguero.

This faction forcefully argued for the immediate restoration of full US economic and military assistance to the Batista regime in quantities sufficient to defeat the rebels. Further, if necessary, the United States should introduce its military forces to ensure a Cuban government victory. Despite the potentially high diplomatic costs associated with a US military response, these officials believed that every other policy option ran the greater risk of permitting communism in Cuba.

The Central Intelligence Agency's view of the Cuban situation occupied a middle ground between the two State Department factions. The CIA was convinced that a rebel victory in Cuba would inevitably threaten American interests. Although available evidence did not indicate Communist domination of the 26th of July Movement, Communist influence was evident and Castro's control over the movement was not considered strong enough to prevent the

Communists from using the 26th of July Movement to advance their own agenda. Further, the agency predicted that the longer Castro's forces were unsuccessful in their attempt to oust Batista, the more likely it would be that they would request Communist assistance. The CIA also doubted Castro's willingness to cooperate with his moderate partners in the Civic Revolutionary Front in any post-Batista government. But CIA estimates of the amount of assistance required to shore up the Batista regime suggested that such US action would appear interventionist to Latin Americans and would engender political repercussions extending beyond Cuba.

US intelligence reports at this time did question the ability of the Cuban armed forces to fight the rebels effectively. Nevertheless, these reports concluded that the Cuban opposition would not be able to overthrow the Batista government prior to Rivero Aguero's February 24, 1959, inauguration.

The CIA recommended that the United States provide active support for an anti-Castro opposition government acceptable to US interests, and it even began to make contact with anti-Castro opposition groups. The agency further argued that the only viable provisional government would be a military junta devoid of Batista supporters and pledged to the restoration of democracy; such a regime could win the support of the Cuban people, and only the military was capable of ousting Batista in the short term. The agency admitted that it was unclear whether or under what circumstances the military would undertake this action, but it believed that the United States had sufficient time to pursue this option effectively.

The Defense Department's proposed responses to Batista's deteriorating position resembled those of the State Department's minority faction, but for somewhat different reasons. Concerned about US military interests in Cuba, the Defense Department emphasized the importance of Batista's traditional willingness to accept a continuing US presence at the Guantanamo Bay naval base and maintain Cuba's role as a strong ally against Soviet expansionism in the Caribbean region. The cooperation of the 26th of July Movement, and of Fidel Castro in particular, on these important security matters, by contrast, was considered highly doubtful.

Defense Department personnel also disagreed with the prediction that US military support for Batista would inevitably encounter opposition throughout Latin America. They argued that some Latin American governments would support US action to prevent the Castro-led rebels from coming to power. Defense, therefore, recommended immediate reinstatement of US military assistance to the Batista government.

Congressional perceptions of Cuban events ranged widely--from members who believed that the 26th of July Movement was Communist-dominated to those who felt that the Castro-led rebels were idealistic reformers fighting against a tyrannical regime. Policy proposals ranged just as widely--from strong US military and economic support for the Batista regime to the view that the United States should disassociate itself from Batista and warmly accept a rebel victory.

The great majority of those in Congress, however, took an intermediate position. They believed the United States should distance itself from Latin American dictators as a first step in strengthening regional resistance to Communist infiltration through political and economic development, but they also mistrusted the Castro-led rebels. Consequently, a congressional majority recommended maintaining the arms embargo against Batista without offering support to the rebels. In short, congressional opinion was divided and cautious.

In late November 1958, US-Cuban policy was formulated in a noncrisis atmosphere; decisionmakers shared the belief that the Batista regime would survive at least a few more months. At the same time, President Dwight Eisenhower and Secretary of State John Foster Dulles were preoccupied with US-Soviet relations. As a result, Cuban policy decisions were formulated mainly at middle levels of the various federal bureaucracies; few, if any, high-level officials were directly involved in the decisionmaking process for Cuba at this stage.

Overall, the US response to Batista's declining position was neither assertive nor clear. Policy largely reflected the view of the State Department, but the department itself was divided. Although a majority wanted to establish a third-force government, pursuit of this objective was impeded by concern about appearing to intervene in Cuban affairs.

As a first step toward possible US support for a third-force government, State Department and CIA officials met independently with representatives of several anti-Castro opposition movements during November and December. But American reluctance to be seen as intervening prevented these officials from promising any material assistance.

Fact-Facing and Its Frustrations

In late November, the State Department ordered Ambassador Smith to inform Batista of Washington's conclusion that he was an obstacle to peace and thus should resign the presidency and leave Cuba. But Smith refused to carry out this order until mid-December; he argued that it ran counter to his "basic instructions" from the White House. In frustration, Assistant Secretary Rubottom recalled Smith to Washington to remind him of his instructions.

Smith further insisted that all cable traffic from the US Embassy in Havana to the State Department emphasize evidence of Communist influence in the 26th of July Movement and support his view that the only possible way to avoid communism in Cuba was to renew US military assistance to the Batista regime.

When the American ambassador finally informed Batista that the United States believed his resignation was a necessary first step toward national reconciliation, the department prohibited Smith from discussing the possible make-up of any post-Batista provisional government with the dictator; such a discussion might have been construed as inappropriate US intervention in Cuban affairs. Batista, however, was hesitant to turn power over to a provisional government until he was sure it would not be dominated by his political opponents.

Another US emissary, William Pawley, spoke with Batista in early December about resigning in favor of a civilian-military junta. The State Department opposed Pawley's effort because his specific proposal for the shape of Cuba's political future would appear interventionist. As a compromise, the Pawley mission went forward, but the department prohibited Pawley from informing Batista that he represented the US government. As a private citizen, however, Pawley was unable to overcome Batista's steadfast refusal to resign.

Meanwhile, the CIA, without the knowledge of the State Department, began to lay the groundwork for a US-supported provisional military junta. For its part, the Defense Department exploited its close contacts with the Cuban military to press for the reinstatement of US military assistance to Batista.

Developments in Cuba in December forced decisionmakers to reevaluate US policy once again. Batista's hold on power was deteriorating more rapidly than US intelligence had predicted. By mid-December, the rebels dominated Oriente Province in the east and were active in several other provinces, the Cuban military showed increasing signs of demoralization, and the economy's decline intensified.

Despite Batista's tenuous hold on power and the increasing power and popularity of the rebel opposition, it still appeared to US officials that the regime would last at least another two months. During this time, it was assumed, the United States might be able to engineer a peaceful transition of power advantageous to US interests. Nevertheless, by late December high-level administration officials had become sufficiently concerned with Cuban developments to expand their involvement from simply monitoring Cuban events and bureaucratic responses to direct involvement in the decisionmaking process.

At this time, Acting Secretary of State Christian Herter (who had taken over from the hospitalized John Foster Dulles) sent a memorandum to President Eisenhower describing the Cuban situation, the current US response, and recommending policy changes. As acting secretary, Herter did not have the authority to launch new policy approaches toward Cuba, but he did exert substantial influence over current policy modifications.

Herter's view of Cuban developments reflected his strong belief that underdeveloped countries required socioeconomic and political reforms to prevent domestic unrest and the opportunity it provided for Communist subversion. He thus agreed with the majority of State Department officials that any solution to Cuba's instability required Batista's removal. But the acting secretary also shared the CIA's conclusion, somewhat at odds with the view of most State Department officials, that the 26th of July Movement was under Communist influence, even if it was not Communist-dominated.

Herter's December 23 memorandum to the president reflected these two conclusions. The memorandum addressed what the United States "might appropriately do to encourage a solution short of the bloodbath which could result there [in Cuba]." The acting secretary noted the State Department's conclusion that "any solution in Cuba requires that Batista must relinquish power" and argued that the United States must act decisively, employing "all available means short of outright intervention" to establish a broadly popular third-force government to preempt a Castro victory.

Presidential Involvement

The immediate effect of Christian Herter's memorandum was to involve President Eisenhower and his conceptions of effective policy and procedures in the making of Cuban policy. Eisenhower firmly believed in the utility of a strict chain of command. He did not like to involve himself directly in the day-to-day decisions on foreign policy matters, particularly those independent of US-Soviet relations. He preferred to delegate authority and limit his active involvement in matters he considered routine or the responsibility of the bureaucracy. But once involved, the president did not hesitate to use his authority to determine the future course of US policy.

President Eisenhower's main foreign policy focus throughout his presidency was US-Soviet relations. President Eisenhower shared his advisers' belief that the Soviet Union would take advantage of instability anywhere in the world to expand its international influence relative to the United States. Since political instability was most common in underdeveloped regions, Eisenhower concluded that the underdeveloped countries would become the main battleground between the United States and the Soviet Union. But he did not believe that the United States should respond forcefully to every instance of apparent Soviet meddling in underdeveloped countries. To the contrary, the United States should focus its resources on threats to vital US interests instead of "putting out brush fires" around the world. Further, the United States should act only if a quick, effective way to protect its interests were available; President Eisenhower felt no action was better than an ineffective policy in pursuit of ill-defined objectives. Eisenhower's approach to Latin America reflected these more general perceptions about the nature of Soviet expansionism and the most effective US response. But since Latin America seemed less vulnerable than other underdeveloped regions, particularly the Middle East, the president gave it very little attention.

With regard to foreign policy tactics, President Eisenhower felt that developing constructive relations with other nations, regardless of their internal political course, generally would be the best US policy approach; he believed most disagreements between nations could be resolved through accommodation. When this option was not feasible, the president favored using the minimum pressure necessary to achieve US objectives; he generally opposed the use of US military force except as a last resort. This approach extended to Latin America where, Eisenhower believed, US military intervention had been historically ineffective. But Eisenhower also felt that prudent use of covert operations could effectively advance US interests where military force might otherwise seem appropriate, and he strongly believed in the utility of contingency planning in ambiguous situations.

As his second term progressed, the president became increasingly aware that traditional US development policies for Latin America based on private economic assistance were insufficient to eliminate the economic and political inequities which he believed provided opportunities for Soviet expansionism. By the end of 1958, largely in response to the findings of a recent official trip to Latin America by his brother, Milton, President Eisenhower began to support a more activist role for the US government to promote Latin American political and economic development.

The president was greatly concerned by Herter's conclusion that Batista's demise was imminent and that the United States should "employ all available means short of outright intervention" in support of a third-force government. Eisenhower called an immediate meeting of his National Security Council to discuss the situation in Cuba and US options. Although neither Secretary of State Dulles nor Acting Secretary Herter were present at this December 23 meeting, the contents of Herter's policy memorandum served as the meeting's point of departure.

At a meeting in late December, CIA Director Allen Dulles informed the president that Communists and other radicals had apparently infiltrated the Castro movement. He predicted that such Communists would participate in government in the event of Castro's seizing power. The Defense Department representative apparently concurred; he argued forcefully that the only way to avoid communism in Cuba was to restore full US military support for the Batista regime immediately.

President Eisenhower agreed with the unanimous conclusion of his advisers that the United States should aim to prevent a Castro government. But Eisenhower rejected the argument that the United States should support Batista as the lesser of two evils. Eisenhower believed US military support for Batista would be counterproductive: its ultimate success was highly questionable and it clearly would provoke charges of US interventionism. The president concluded that if Castro were as threatening to US interests as US intelligence suggested, the best option for the United States was to continue the search for an anti-Castro opposition force capable of reestablishing political stability. In addition, Eisenhower directed the State Department to contact the OAS about using its good offices to convince Batista to resign on humanitarian grounds.

DISCUSSION QUESTIONS

1. *How could the United States most effectively exert influence on the character of a post-Batista government? Was a negotiated solution still possible?*
2. *How could Batista be eased out of power?*
3. *Was it still possible at this point to prevent a Castro-led government?*
4. *Was a third-force government still an option? If so, how could the United States go about encouraging creation of such a government? What were the probable risks and costs in taking such an initiative?*

REVOLUTION AND ACCOMMODATION

Castro Takes Over

In the early hours of January 1, 1959, Fulgencio Batista took the initiative and abruptly fled Cuba. He left behind a power vacuum that only the Castro-led revolutionaries appeared able to fill, thereby eliminating immediate prospects for a third-force government.

To preempt any attempt by Batista and his supporters to install a pliant replacement regime, the rebels immediately called a general strike that effectively closed down the Cuban economy. The success of this strike, and Castro's ensuing "Triumphal March" across Cuba in which the revolutionary leader received an enthusiastic welcome at every stop, demonstrated extensive popular support for Castro throughout the country. During this period of national euphoria the revolution rapidly consolidated its control over the nation.

The type of government the revolutionaries would bring to Cuba, however, remained unclear. Castro's political leanings, as presented in his July 1957 "Political-Social Manifesto from the Sierra Maestra," appeared essentially reformist. The manifesto proposed free elections, constitutional government, agrarian reform, increased industrialization, and opposition to foreign intervention. But Castro's subsequent proclamations made fewer references to constitutional democracy and were more radical in tone. Also, US intelligence reports of Castro's earlier political statements and his past involvement in political violence concluded that he was a fervent nationalist, harbored authoritarian tendencies, and strongly opposed US domination of the Cuban economy and Cuban culture.

On January 2, Castro fulfilled his promise to appoint the moderate Manuel Urrutia as provisional president. Urrutia then appointed a number of political moderates, including some highly respected individuals, along with several radicals to serve in his cabinet. It appeared, therefore, that power would be divided between political moderates, on the one hand, and Castro and his more radical supporters, on the other. The long-term balance of this division of power, however, was uncertain. Further, President Urrutia's apparent indecisiveness and the inexperience of many officials in the new government generated concern in Washington about the effectiveness of this government--US officials believed a weak government could provide an opportunity for Communist meddling. But the provisional government seemed generally friendly to the United States, though it professed to be neither pro-American nor pro-Communist, and had stated its willingness to fulfill its international and regional obligations. In addition, the new government's proposed land reform and expropriation policies were fairly moderate.

Fidel Castro's January 2 victory speech also painted an ambiguous picture of Cuba's future. Castro generated some concern in Washington by stating that on this occasion the revolution would take charge, rather than (as in 1898) yielding power to the United States. He further declared that the revolution was just beginning and that success would not be an easy task. But Castro also indicated that civil rights and freedom of the press would be restored and the rights of foreigners and their property would be fully respected. Further, on January 5, the *New York Times* quoted Che Guevarra, one of the rebel leaders the CIA believed to be a Communist sympathizer, as stating, "I have never been a Communist. Dictators always say their enemies are Communists, and it gave me a pain to be called an international Communist all the time."

US Responses

The precipitous end of the Batista regime and the resulting potential for Cuban political instability disturbed US decisionmakers. In the country at large, the fairy tale quality of the rebels' sudden and relatively bloodless victory over the repressive Batista regime generated considerable goodwill for the new government.

But this sentiment, as represented in the media, did not so much reflect support for Fidel Castro personally as sympathy for the victory of the Cuban people against a repressive dictatorship. Some newspapers at this time did argue that the new government was either Communist or susceptible to Communist subversion, but the vast majority of media opinion expressed either cautious approval or full support for the revolutionary regime. Even some American businessmen in Cuba urged rapid US recognition of the new government, arguing that it appeared to be far better than anything they had dared hoped for.

Washington, however, was concerned that a revolutionary government would also be revolutionary where the traditional structure of US-Cuban relations was concerned. Castro's policy statements did suggest that such changes were very likely, but they left it unclear how far they would go. American policymakers seemed to believe that the durability of close US-Cuban relations would ensure that any problems connected with Batista's departure could be worked out, sooner or later.

The initial US response to the Cuban revolutionary regime reflected two distinct decisionmaking processes operating in early January 1959. Within the

State Department, policy continued to reflect the majority's distrust of Fidel Castro and their uncertainty about the long-term compatibility with fundamental US national interests of the radical ideas espoused by Castro and his close associates. But these officials did not believe that a Castro-led government would inevitably threaten US interests since much of the radical rhetoric seemed to reflect the revolutionaries' inexperience and intoxication with victory. Once the revolutionaries were faced with the task of governing, the reality of Cuba's economic and geographic dependence on the United States would force moderation in their rhetoric and policy proposals.

Further, a Castro-led government did not appear inevitable. The moderates within the new government appeared capable of consolidating their power at Castro's expense, and even if they failed to take control of the government, their presence seemed likely to temper the more radical components of Castro's political program.

Three additional factors influenced State Department thinking. The department majority believed that an expansion of Soviet influence into Cuba was very unlikely because of Cuba's proximity to the United States. Consequently, the United States should have sufficient time and latitude to reach an accommodation of interests with the new Cuban regime. The new regime also had met the basic US requirements for diplomatic recognition, including an expressed willingness to fulfill its international obligations and to favor democracy over communism. In addition, State Department standard decision procedures helped mute the views of officials who were skeptical about the new men in Havana.

Among such dissenters, only Ambassador Smith was in a position to influence US policy. Convinced that the 26th of July Movement was Communist-dominated, Smith instructed Embassy personnel to forward any evidence of Communist inclinations in the new regime to the State Department in order to convince Washington that it was unwise to recognize the new regime until its true character had emerged. Smith also tried to convince his superiors that the United States should not appoint a new ambassador to Cuba; to do so, he said, would seem to acknowledge--wrongly, in Smith's view--that previous US policy toward Cuba had been ill-conceived.

But Ambassador Smith had little impact, partly because of the way in which the State Department was making policy at this time. In a series of meetings between Smith and high-level department officials who sharply disagreed with the Ambassador's view of Cuban events, Smith found himself outranked and outnumbered.

Despite misgivings about the new regime, the State Department informed the president that US interests in Cuba would best be protected by establishing productive relations with the new government. The department further argued that the divided political character of the new regime called for a generally accommodating policy designed to strengthen the moderates. But-- it suggested--this policy should be combined with careful attention to Cuban developments that might identify the likely future orientation of the regime. Specifically, the United States should watch for Communists in the government, policies damaging to US interests, anti-American domestic policies, movement toward neutrality in the Cold War, reduced support for the inter-American system, and increased state control of the economy.

Finally, the department recommended replacing Ambassador Smith as a first step in implementing its proposed policy, given Smith's close ties to the Batista government. The United States should appoint an individual more sympathetic to the objectives of revolutionary regimes in order to indicate the willingness of the United States to establish a positive relationship with the new government.

The cabinet-level decisionmaking process also influenced the initial US response to the Cuban revolutionary regime. President Eisenhower's top advisers exhibited only limited concern that the rebel victory might have significant negative consequences for US-Cuban relations. Although anxious about the quality of US relations with the rebel government, these officials concluded that the new regime posed no imminent strategic threat. At the same time, other international developments, including the unresolved Berlin crisis, were threatening US strategic interests and thus required presidential attention.

President Eisenhower's personal attitude toward Batista's sudden departure was influenced partly by his general preference for accommodation and his bias toward nonintervention in hemispheric affairs, but it also reflected his view that extended instability in Cuba would create an opportunity for Communist meddling 90 miles from the US border. Eisenhower believed that Cuba's internal defenses against communism could be reinforced by moderate social and political reforms, but inconclusive intelligence reports regarding the likely future policy course of the revolutionaries left the president less certain than the State Department about the willingness of the new Cuban government to pursue a reformist path.

DISCUSSION QUESTIONS

1. *What were the main dilemmas confronting US policymakers in the wake of Batista's departure?*

2.   *What obstacles did policymakers face?*
3.   *How "rational" was US policy at this time?*

FURTHER READING ON CUBA

Books

Blasier, Cole. *The Hovering Giant*. Pittsburgh: University of Pittsburgh Press, 1979.

Bonsal, Philip W. *Cuba, Castro, and the United States*. Pittsburgh: University of Pittsburgh Press, 1971.

Halperin, Maurice. *The Rise and Decline of Fidel Castro*. Berkeley: University of California Press, 1972.

Smith, Earl E.T. *The Fourth Floor*. New York: Random House, 1962.

Szulc, Tad. *Fidel: A Critical Portrait*. New York: Morrow, 1986.

Welch, Richard. *Response to Revolution: The United States and the Cuban Revolution, 1959-1961*. Chapel Hill: University of North Carolina Press, 1985.

Articles

Gonzalez, Edward. "Castro's Revolution, Cuban Communist Appeals, and Soviet Response." *World Politics* 21, 1 (1968): 39-68.

3

NICARAGUA, 1978–1979
The Fall of
Anastasio Somoza Debayle

The second case deals with another crisis in the Western hemisphere, involving the downfall of another American-supported dictator under pressure from another radical, guerrilla movement. Specifically, it describes the collapse in 1978-1979 of the regime of President Anastasio Somoza Debayle of Nicaragua and the seizure of power by the Marxist-oriented Sandinista National Liberation Front (FSLN--generally known as the "Sandinistas").

This story has obvious similarities to that of the expulsion of Batista by Fidel Castro. It shows US policymakers confronting similar dilemmas and experiencing similar conflicts. But the international context is different. The crisis occurs in the aftermath of the Vietnam War, at a time of serious division within the American political establishment over the objectives to be pursued in foreign policy and the kinds of diplomatic and military commitments to be undertaken in pursuing these objectives. Here we see a complicated and distinctive pattern of division among policymakers, especially between "interventionist" and "noninterventionist" liberals (as well as the more familiar conflict between "Cold Warriors" and those intent on respecting national boundaries and sensibilities).

This chapter is primarily the work of Douglas A. Chalmers as presented in his case study, Nicaragua, 1978-1979: The United States and Anastasio Somoza--Dealing with Friendly Dictators Who Are Losing Their Authority, *Pew case study no. 105, with additional material inserted by the editor from other cases and from secondary sources as indicated in the notes.*

This case also illustrates (as the Cuban case does not) the problems of negotiating an acceptable arrangement for a transition in power where the parties are already locked in conflict. It offers a chance to examine both the problems of mediating in such conflicts and the limits of American power in influencing, much less controlling, the process of expulsion from and seizure of power in foreign countries.

* * *

On January 10, 1978, Pedro Joaquin Chamorro, the lively and combative editor of the most important newspaper in Nicaragua, *La Prensa*, was driving to work in one of the many areas of Managua still not rebuilt after the massive earthquake six years earlier. Armed men suddenly jumped from a truck that blocked his way and opened fire, killing him. Within hours, President Anastasio Somoza announced the arrest and confession of a man who said he had been paid by a businessman whom Chamorro's paper had attacked for shady deals. However, few believed Somoza's claim that the killing was not political. Many thought Somoza himself must be implicated. The identity of the killers was never established to everyone's satisfaction. A major political crisis followed.

THE STATUS QUO

Nicaraguan Politics

By early 1978, Nicaragua, which had been ruled by the Somoza family for some forty years, found itself contemplating an uncertain future. This situation was not unfamiliar to the people of Nicaragua; throughout the nineteenth century sharp economic and political cleavages had resulted in repeated armed clashes. Most notorious was the intervention in the 1850s by Central American conservatives who were attempting to oust William Walker, an American adventurer who had been invited to Nicaragua by the liberals to fight the landed elite.[1]

Direct American intervention occurred on several occasions over the subsequent eighty years. In 1910, for example, President Taft ordered 2,600 US marines into Nicaragua to squash a revolt against President Diaz (who had transferred to New York bankers the ownership of Nicaragua's Nation Bank,

51 percent of its railroads, and its customs collector, in order to obtain a $10 million loan).[2]

The American intervention ensured Diaz five years of rule. A US military presence, however, continued until early 1930s. But US military and economic presence did not bring tranquility. In 1927, the Liberal party, backed by Mexico and led by General Augusto Cesar Sandino, launched a revolt that lasted some six years. Washington, realizing that its image had been badly tarnished by its tendency to intervene militarily whenever its will in the Caribbean Basin was challenged and recognizing that its military presence in Nicaragua had become too costly, withdrew its troops in 1933.[3]

This action did not signify that Washington was surrendering control; it merely reflected a change in tactics. Prior to sailing its troops home, Washington had helped form the Nicaraguan National Guard, under the leadership of Anastasio Somoza Garcia. Both actions proved to be far-reaching. First, hostilities came to an end almost immediately; second, Sandino, whose central goal had been to expel the United States and help end hostilities, was assassinated in 1934 when his goals were finally achieved; and finally, Somoza Garcia took over the reins of government in 1936, with the full support of Nicaragua's upper class. This last action proved to be the beginning of the Somoza dynasty.[4]

Somoza Garcia ruled until he was assassinated in 1956. His oldest son, Luis, replaced him in the presidential palace in 1957, while Anastasio, Jr. ("Tacho"), controlled the National Guard. In 1963, Rene Schick became president after Luis had decided that it would be politically prudent to obey the constitutional requirement that the office not be occupied by the same person for more than one term. The move was merely a symbolic gesture. Tacho remained commander of the National Guard, and the Somoza family continued to dominate the economic and political arenas. Ownership of land and industry became further concentrated during the 1960s, with the Somozas sitting at the top. Moreover, the political arena was fully dominated by the Nationalist Liberal party, which remained under the control of one Somoza or another.[5]

The political system the Somozas built was much like the politics of the big city bosses in the United States in the early part of the century. Formally adhering to a constitution with the full set of guarantees of free competition and individual rights, the system managed to give enormous power and permanence to the group in power. The regime was illiberal without being totalitarian. It allowed critics "a relatively large amount of space to act in public life," so long as they did not challenge the Somozas' hold on power.[6] Elite opposition was tolerated, particularly when it was expressed in a press that did not

reach far into the largely illiterate population. Serious opposition was sometimes dealt with by discreet brutality behind closed doors or, if it were on a
larger scale, through special "states of emergency" that gave the National
Guard the right to ignore constitutional guarantees.

Political and economic repression did not remain unopposed. Between
1959 and 1961, a wave of armed challenges to the Somoza government broke
out. The National Guard had little difficulty in crushing the rebellion, but it
could not destroy the commitment of some of the rebels to end the Somozas'
rule. In 1961, veteran leftists from variety of backgrounds formed the FSLN.

The threat posed by this new organization remained low. In 1964, the
Central Intelligence Agency concluded that the FSLN was not "a serious threat
to the government." But the challenge was not just one from the left.
Although the sounds of strain on the right had remained almost inaudible
during the early 1960s, in 1966 they became much louder. By then, economic
progress had virtually come to a halt, the balance of payments had worsened,
and unemployment had increased. Elections were scheduled for 1966, and the
opposition united behind the candidacy of the Conservative leader Fernando
Aguero. With editorial support from Pedro Joaquin Chamorro through *La
Prensa*, Aguero promised land reforms and a more equitable political and
social structure.[7]

Aguero and Chamorro were too weak to defeat Somoza and the support
he received from the United States. But this new victory did not reduce the
opposition, both constitutional and extraconstitutional. Its next opportunity
came in the form of a natural disaster. In December 1972, a major earthquake hit Managua, killing some 10,000 people and destroying homes,
commercial businesses, and small industries. The United States responded
immediately by sending $32 million for reconstruction. But this rescue opera-
tion did not bring about the hoped-for recovery. Mismanagement and corruption, along with the increase in price of energy which resulted from the 1973
OPEC oil embargo, provoked popular mobilization. In addition, in 1974 the
Somoza regime began to face something it assumed had been successfully
suppressed: hostile armed opposition.[8]

Although the guerrilla activities of the FSLN had not been a match for
Somoza's National Guard, on occasion they were quite effective in capturing
world attention. On December 27, 1974, for instance, the FSLN took a large
group of hostages from guests at a cocktail party being given in honor of US
Ambassador Turner B. Shelton. The commando group demanded, among
other things, the release of all political prisoners, $5 million, and the immedi-
ate and complete publication of a communique. Somoza gave in to the

Sandinistas' demands in spite of pressure from hardliners within the National Guard.[9]

Within the guerrilla movement itself, the attack and the repression Somoza launched in its wake unleashed a sharp debate on tactics, with the result that the FSLN split into three groups in 1975, constituting something of a catalogue of revolutionary strategies. First, there was the "Proletarian Tendency," which rejected theatrical moves aimed at sudden victories and dedicated itself to classic Marxist organization of a predominantly urban working class. The "Prolonged Popular War" faction also criticized the cocktail party episode and concentrated on mobilization among the peasants in a strategy often called Maoist. This group held that the Somoza regime lacked the capability and the will to conduct and survive a long war. The "Insurrectionists," most often known as the "Third Way" (*Terceristas*), were mainly responsible for the Christmas party attack and advocated appeals to the widest possible base of anti-Somoza groups in order to stimulate an early overthrow of the dictator.

With these divisions (and the death of a principal founder of the FSLN, Carlos Fonseca), US intelligence officers were right to assume that the greatest threat to the Somoza regime was not the Sandinistas. Rather, the ability of Somoza to govern was being undermined principally by Nicaragua's political moderates, specifically, the Catholic Church and businessmen outside the Somoza network. Both were vocal in protesting human rights violations committed by the government and in calling for the creation of a political system that would promote "freedom, justice, and equality."[10]

The Church, while never close to Somoza, dropped its relative passivity when Miguel Obando y Bravo became Archbishop of Managua in 1970. The new head of the Nicaraguan Church began to demonstrate a willingness to stand up to Somoza, refusing the president's gift of a Mercedes-Benz and publicly calling attention to abuses of the regime. At the parish level, young priests drew support from the decisions of Vatican II and Liberation Theology and began to organize study groups and popular education schemes with social and antidictatorial content, as they had all over Latin America.

Many businessmen not linked tightly to the huge Somoza family holdings also became restive. Thus in March 1974 a meeting was organized by a group of businessmen called the Superior Council of Private Initiative (COSIP), representing the bulk of business interests outside of the Somoza family group. COSIP distributed a statement sharply critical of Somoza's handling of the reconstruction. It was the first time that such a public denunciation of Somoza had been made by an elite group not associated with the traditional Conservative faction.

The United States and the Somoza Dynasty

In the 1930s and 1940s, many American policymakers, while despising Somoza as an avaricious dictator, acknowledged that he was doing effectively what the marines had failed to do, namely, ensuring continuity and encouraging economic growth. They therefore chose to use the high-sounding phrase "nonintervention" to justify their tolerance of a harsh regime. This attitude of weary pragmatism was perfectly expressed in President Roosevelt's reported comment on Somoza: "He's a sonofabitch, but he's ours." In May 1939, with World War II looming, Somoza was invited for a state visit to Washington. Pictures show him and Roosevelt in top hats riding in the streets of the US capital. (Somoza was more impressed by his reception than he should have been: The American government was "using the arrangements as a dress rehearsal for a visit by British royalty."[11])

In external relations, the Somoza family was always careful to meet Washington's minimum requirements. The elder Somoza suppressed disruptive political movements and promoted economic growth. As World War II approached and the United States assumed worldwide responsibilities, he further assured himself of US backing by meticulous support for American foreign policy. When World War II broke out, he declared war on Germany and Italy (expropriating the property of German and Italian citizens, which he subsequently sold for a large profit).

During the high period of the Cold War, the Somozas were always available to help in squashing possible outbreaks of communism in their region. In 1954, for example, the US government became worried by Guatemala's expropriation of United Fruit property and toleration of some Communists in the government of Jacobo Arbenz. The Nicaraguan government provided a secret staging ground for the CIA-run coup against Arbenz.

Anastasio Somoza Garcia, like his sons, also sought out and made friends among Americans. Many liked his rough-and-ready style and thought of him as the best defense against chaos, threats to property, Nazism, and communism. Somoza, like many other upper-class Nicaraguans, often visited the United States and sent his sons, Luis and Anastasio, there to study. It was often said that the sons, particularly Anastasio, Jr., who went to LaSalle Military Academy on Long Island and then West Point, knew the United States better than Nicaragua, and the English language better than Spanish.

In Central America itself, the dynasty had a mixture of enemies and allies. After World War II, Somoza, Sr., faced a group of presidents--Juan Jose Arevalo of Guatemala, Jose Figueres of Costa Rica, and Romulo Betancourt of Venezuela--who had themselves installed democratic governments after successful uprisings against dictators and who were openly hostile to Somoza. They sponsored the shadowy group called the Caribbean Legion, an antidictatorial alliance that targeted Somoza, along with Batista in Cuba and Trujillo in the Dominican Republic.

In 1959, Batista fled and a stridently anti-American regime emerged in Cuba. In May 1960, Trujillo was assassinated and a period of instability followed. Fearing a seizure of power by Communist sympathizers, the Johnson administration dispatched American forces to the Dominican Republic in 1965. The younger Somozas responded to such events as their father would have done--offering aid (both open and covert) to worried American policymakers. When the United States organized an expeditionary force to invade Cuba at the Bay of Pigs in 1961, Nicaragua again provided a base for operations. The Somozas offered to send planes to bomb Castro's forces.

In 1965, Nicaragua was one of the few countries in Latin America providing troops for OAS-sponsored, but US-directed, action in the Dominican Republic. Somoza's eagerness to help the United States took a more expansive turn in 1967, when Tacho offered to send troops to that country. The offer was turned down with thanks.

Tacho, moreover, followed his father's tradition of personal ingratiation with American officials. There were those in the State Department who distrusted the younger Somoza, but US messages to Managua were delivered by ambassadors such as Thomas E. Whelan and Turner B. Shelton, political appointees who liked the backslapping, hard-drinking, and card-playing style of the Somozas.

The younger Somoza did not limit his friendship to diplomats. He maintained close friendships with several congressmen, notably John Murphy (D-NY, and a former classmate at LaSalle Military Academy) and Charles Wilson (D-TX). From time to time he hired professional lobbyists among the Washington legal and political community. Nicaragua was kept off the front pages and contacts were behind closed doors.

Somoza also continued the close relations with the US military that had begun with the marines in the 1920s. He kept in contact with his West Point graduating class and worked closely with the American officers in the US Southern Command, based in Panama. Indeed, the most tangible sign of US support for the dynasty was military aid, which helped to keep the National Guard a strong and well-equipped force.[12]

The habit of looking to Washington was not, however, limited to the Somozas. Nicaraguan politicians of all kinds saw alliance with the United States as desirable or necessary to win internal political struggles. Though intellectuals and a few political figures rejected such dependent thinking, even

Sandino reportedly twice offered to "lay down his arms if the US military would take over the Nicaraguan government and run it until the next elections."[13] Both government and opposition figures sought out the American Ambassador for advice or approval of their actions.

The Carter Administration

The election of Jimmy Carter as president of the United States in 1976 brought a new group into power in Washington and a new set of policies that strongly affected Nicaragua. Of these, the most important concerned human rights. After the international and domestic debacles of Vietnam and Watergate, in which amoral power politics seemed to have taken precedence over principle, and to have failed, the Carter administration sought a new direction.

The defense of basic human rights offered an alternative to total withdrawal from the world. Carter and his advisers hoped that Americans could agree on such active idealism after more than a decade of internal political conflicts. Anti-communism could be redefined and reemphasized by support for Jews and dissidents in the Soviet Union and attacks on the absence of elections and free expression elsewhere in the Soviet Bloc.

The human rights policies also provided a point of departure for what was hoped to be a more acceptable kind of intervention in the anti-Communist, but embarrassingly antidemocratic Latin American military regimes. Yet applying human rights policies to Nicaragua was no simple or obvious task. It had had forty years of one-man rule rather than a decade of the faceless and austere bureaucratic authoritarianism of South American states such as Brazil and Argentina. Personal rule might appear easier to curb because of the exposed position of the leader. But it was also a type of rule that involved long-standing networks of obligations and dependencies that were complicated to break. With personal power went a kind of corruption, complete with networks of payoffs. Human rights abuses were often entangled with these sorts of deals.

Further, the longevity of the dictatorship meant that neither the opposition nor the government's supporters had any traditions, organizations, or institutions for conducting the kind of legally guaranteed political competition that is a prerequisite for the protection of rights. The opposition tradition of Nicaragua was dominated by people such as Sandino, a long series of Conservatives up to Pedro Joaquin Chamorro, and the Sandinistas, all of whom had placed heavy emphasis on armed rebellion. "Reforming" Nicaragua inevitably meant a far more complete reconstruction of the political system than in Brazil or Argentina, where there was a historical memory, however tenuous, of democratic institutions. The legal structure of Nicaragua had long been subject to manipulation, and the beginnings of opposition organization were only that--beginnings.

The human rights campaign made a dramatic change in the setting of Washington's policymaking toward Nicaragua. For many years, Somoza's well-placed friends had been able to fend off attacks in an atmosphere of general indifference. But by the mid-1970s the cast of characters seeking to influence US policy toward Nicaragua, and the arenas where that policy was hammered out, had become more complex.

Human rights-oriented think tanks and lobbying groups hostile to dictatorial regimes had emerged, first working on Congress, and then more and more successfully on the new administration. Congress, long chiefly the scene of quiet but effective pro-Somoza activity, became the arena of anti-Somoza activists as well. Political figures such as Representative Ed Koch (D-NY) and Senator Frank Church (D-ID) were prominent in publicly criticizing Nicaragua and Somoza. Somoza, in turn, hired professional public relations firms, such as Sullivan, Sarria and Associates of Ft. Lauderdale, Florida, and lobbyists such as Fred Korth, former secretary of the navy, and William Cramer (R), eight-term representative from Florida. Policy toward Nicaragua was being more widely debated both in the US government and in the press.

American diplomacy toward Nicaragua, indeed, underwent a transformation, the effects of which were apparent even before 1977. Despite the complacency of ambassadors like Shelton, criticism began to flow thinly through official channels, largely thanks to a single foreign service officer, James Cheek, who filed detailed reports through a separate "dissent" channel to the State Department. Cheek's assessments often contradicted those of his ambassador.[14]

With the resignation of President Nixon, Secretary of State Henry Kissinger successfully induced William D. Rogers, former deputy coordinator of the Alliance for Progress in the Kennedy administration, to become the new assistant secretary of state for inter-American affairs. Rogers insisted on replacing Ambassador Shelton with someone who would be less identified with Somoza.[15]

Shelton's successor was James D. Theberge, a conservative academic specialist on Soviet penetration of Latin America. Theberge widened the Embassy's range of contacts with the opposition, although not with the guerrillas. Somoza later commented in his account of the period: "our first visit,

Mr. Theberge told me that he had been advised by the State Department to keep his distance from me. This came as a shock and it was hard to take. Next to Nicaragua, I loved the US more than any place in the world. But I had been told by the new Ambassador that he should keep distance between us. I thought, whom in the State Department have I offended?"[16]

By 1977, it was quite clear whom he had offended. Somoza was not, however, immediately worried by the change in climate. His self-confidence was all too apparent in his reaction to the bad news brought from Washington by Adolfo Calero, a Conservative leader who remained on speaking terms with the dictator. Calero reported: "I told Tacho, 'You're going to lose your best friends, the gringos. They say that they're going to make life impossible for you. They are going to try and get your ass.' He said, 'Aw, you think I have no friends in Washington. I can take care of Carter.'"[17]

The Carter administration's agenda itself provided opportunities for Somoza and his North American friends to turn the tables on human rights activists, for complicating and overshadowing decisions about Nicaragua was another policy initiative. Carter had made a commitment to conclude treaties with Panama governing the transfer of the Panama Canal to that country. This was a popular policy in Latin America but was seriously divisive in the United States. Carter was sharply criticized by conservatives for "wanting to give away the Canal." To win support, these critics attacked the government of President Torrijos of Panama as dictatorial.

Carter was strongly committed to the Panama Canal treaties, but to win their approval in the Congress he had to avoid excessively antagonizing the conservatives. To win acceptance of a politically workable treaty from Torrijos he had to avoid including Panama in any broad campaign for human rights.

The debates on Nicaraguan policy and the Panama Canal treaties moved forward simultaneously. Nicaragua was a sideshow, as it had been for decades. Many in Washington were in fact still untroubled by conditions in Nicaragua. At a colloquium on Central America sponsored by the State Department in January 1977 the FSLN was, according to Shirley Christian, "written off as small and of little threat to the Somoza family"--an assessment that led a field service officer newly appointed to the Nicaragua desk to seek another assignment.[18]

In any case, Carter had staked a great many more of his political chips on Panama, and Somoza's allies in Congress were able to make the most of it. In the summer of 1977, Koch and a narrow majority of a committee in the House cut Nicaragua out of a bill for military assistance--an action obviously in tune with the new human rights policies. But Somoza's supporters managed to reverse this in the final vote.

Events in Nicaragua itself at first seemed to confirm the impression of Somoza's invulnerability. On July 28, 1977, Somoza had a heart attack and flew to Miami for treatment. Despite Washington's growing coolness to his regime, nothing much happened while he was gone, at least on the surface. The country was still under the martial law imposed in 1974. Somoza was able to return six weeks later with no apparent political difficulty.

On September 19, Somoza felt politically strong enough to lift martial law and press censorship in what was clearly a gesture toward the Carter administration. The announcement was timed to coincide with the appointment of another new American ambassador, Mauricio Solaun, a Cuban emigre from the pre-Castro period and a University of Illinois sociologist with a cautious manner and little experience in government affairs. Solaun presented his credentials with a message from Carter urging adherence to human rights principles. Solaun persisted in expanding American contacts with the opposition. However, the one group left out was the Sandinistas who in the summer of 1977 were still thought by the CIA to number "fewer than two hundred."

Foreign assumptions about the situation in Nicaragua were shattered by a new wave of opposition activity in the fall. Freed of censorship, *La Prensa* published a call for Somoza's resignation. On October 13, a faction of the FSLN launched a series of coordinated attacks around the country. In Costa Rica during the same month, a committee of Nicaraguan businessmen and intellectual leaders in exile, including at least one member who had been close to the *Terceristas*, announced its opposition to Somoza. The group concerned became known as The Twelve (*Los Doce*) and its members began an international lobbying effort for the overthrow of Somoza. Soon thereafter the Committee for National Dialogue was formed in Managua, including Archbishop Obando y Bravo and Alfonso Robelo, a businessman who had played a key role in the criticism of Somoza after the 1972 earthquake. The committee announced its intention of negotiating with Somoza in order to get him to step down early and hold elections. In December it met with Somoza, but he did not respond to its proposals.

Observing this activity, Solaun and his colleagues at the Managua Embassy concluded that, while it was necessary for Somoza to go, it would be impossible simply to sweep away the political network created by the Somoza dynasty and hope to see a centrist regime emerge. They therefore pressed Washington to adopt a strategy that would involve cooperation with Somoza's party (the Nationalist Liberal party) and the constitutional opposition to ensure the removal of the Somoza clan before Tacho's presidential term expired (in 1981). Solaun himself tried to argue for this approach[19] (called *somocismo sin Somoza*) before Deputy Secretary of State Warren Christopher and other senior officials. But Solaun was an academic by background, not a Washington "insider," and his presentation was ineffective. Most of his listeners decided that the problem was "not worthy of their attention."[20]

With the assassination of Pedro Joaquin Chamorro on January 10, 1978, the problem moved abruptly closer to their attention.

DISCUSSION QUESTIONS

1. *How did the murder of Chamorro change the political situation within Nicaragua?*
2. *How did it change the choices open to Somoza and the United States government?*
3. *To what extent did the US government have, at this point, an accurate appraisal of the situation in Nicaragua?*
4. *Should the US government have paid more attention to the Nicaraguan problem?*
5. *Should it* at this stage *have been more active in approaching opposition groups, including the FSLN? What might it have proposed and sought in communications with the opposition?*

THE REGIME UNDER ATTACK

With the murder of Chamorro, the character of the opposition began to change. First, efforts at negotiated settlement broke down, at least temporarily. The Committee for National Dialogue cancelled its meetings with Somoza, as Chamorro supporters refused to sit down with the man they considered his murderer. Second, more and more people were willing to actively show their opposition. During the next two weeks there were many demonstrations, organized and unorganized. A general strike was called by a loosely organized group, the *Union Democratica de Liberacion* (UDEL), which included businessmen and labor unions, as well as Conservatives.

Finally, armed rebellion was being initiated by people other than the traditional elite opposition and the middle-class intellectuals who formed the guerrillas. In the Monimbo section of Masaya, not far from Managua, the National Guard brutally disrupted a demonstration following a mass held in honor of Chamorro. People in the area found arms and resisted, leading to days of violent conflict and weeks of sporadic fighting. Sandinistas were quick to join the rebels, beginning a practice of supplying leadership to spontaneous rebellions. On their own the FSLN launched a series of attacks on National Guard outposts around the country. Revived in strength after the repression of 1975 and 1976, the FSLN was rapidly becoming synonymous with organized, armed resistance to Somoza. And armed force was becoming increasingly important as an arbiter of events.

Somoza responded with aggressive declarations of his resolve to stay in power, stronger and more violent counterattacks by the National Guard. He also made efforts to find ways of winning back stronger support from the United States, arguing that his struggle was against Cuban-support Communist guerrillas, that stepping down would lead to civil war, and that the United States owed support to their faithful ally.

The US Embassy was approached by Nicaraguan businessmen urging it to pressure Somoza to resign. Many actively sought a stronger US role in finding a new solution. Some were worried that the FSLN might be in a position to step into a vacuum if Somoza hung on and then collapsed.

Arguments in Washington

The turmoil that followed the assassination forced high-level policymakers in the Carter administration to deal with Nicaragua for the first time. Policy toward the country was still the responsibility of an array of diverse officials usually preoccupied with other, apparently more pressing affairs. (For example, the assassination of Chamorro had taken place the day after an outbreak of violence considered the opening of the Iranian revolution.) Making policy on emerging issues like the Nicaraguan crisis involved bringing together representatives from a variety of agencies.

As with most foreign policy questions, principal responsibility was divided in complex and shifting ways between the National Security Council, led by National Security Adviser Zbigniew Brzezinski, and the State Department, then under the leadership of Secretary Cyrus Vance. The latter, at least at this time, had the major responsibility for implementation. The CIA, headed by Stansfield Turner, was important as a main source of information and estimates on the situation in Nicaragua. Later, when the possibility of military intervention was brought up, the Defense Department and the joint chiefs became more actively involved.

Congress played a significant role as a channel for pro- and anti-Somoza lobbying, but was formally involved in the decisionmaking process only when questions of military and economic aid were involved. Giving and withholding aid was the most important material leverage the United States had in Nicaragua, and decisions were often made with the possible reactions of Congress in mind. But at this stage, with considerable aid already in the pipeline, the executive could make considerable short-term changes by suspending or accelerating money flows. Its decisions focused on the attitude to take toward Somoza, what to tell him, with whom else in Nicaragua and the region to deal, and what public positions to take. In this period, no congressional figures became key actors.

Vance and Brzezinski themselves were rarely actively engaged over Nicaraguan matters until the very end, and responsibility fell largely on National Security Council (NSC) and State Department staff who specialized in Latin America. At the NSC, Robert Pastor, a young student of American foreign policy with some experience in the region, had come in with Carter as the NSC's director of Latin American and Caribbean affairs. Pastor urged some measure of pressure to democratize the political system and promote human rights, without overt intervention in the politics of the country.

At the Department of State, the officer formally responsible for Latin American affairs was Terence Todman, a career diplomat with experience chiefly in Africa, who had been named assistant secretary for inter-American affairs. About the time of Chamorro's assassination, he was being eased out for his sometimes all-too-public skepticism about the active posture implied by the human rights policies. The events of the spring of 1978 were taking place in an interim period before a new assistant secretary was appointed.

State's channel to the field included the State Department Desk for Nicaragua, the Bureau for Inter-American Affairs, and Ambassador Solaun. The desk officer in Washington urged a relatively active role in Nicaragua to find some solution through mediation between Somoza and the opposition.

A new actor at State, with an importance lent by Carter's human rights policy, was the Bureau of Human Rights and Humanitarian Affairs headed by Under Secretary of State Pat Derian and her assistant Mark Schneider. In general, they pressed for a focus on Somoza's abuses of human rights, using publicity and threats of withdrawal of aid as the main instruments of influence.

Deputy Secretary of State Warren Christopher had come to play a major role in coordinating Latin American and human rights policy for Vance. It was Christopher who convened a meeting on February 15 of the major actors to discuss policy toward Nicaragua in the wake of the Chamorro assassination. The occasion was not events in Nicaragua directly, but rather a letter to

Carter from Venezuelan President Carlos Andres Perez urging collective action, including pressure on Somoza to allow a visit by the Inter-American Human Rights Commission. Perez, as president of a major oil-producing country, was an important figure to Carter and someone whom Carter sought as an ally in several major foreign policy questions, including the Cuban role in the Horn of Africa.

Knowing what to do required answers to some difficult questions. Could Somoza hold out against the mounting opposition? Could the National Guard, still the best equipped military force in Nicaragua, reestablish control? Were the Sandinistas an effective military force with popular support, or were they simply a set of isolated armed bands? If the Sandinistas were likely to be important, what (if anything) would keep them in a moderate coalition friendly to the United States? Was there any centrist opposition group that could do any better at controlling the situation than Somoza? Depending on the answers to these questions, there were several possible courses of US action.

One possibility was to mute the effort to "reform" Somoza and to increase military and economic aid to support his struggle against the Communist guerrillas. Somoza's friends in the US Congress were urging this course of action. Given the president's commitment to human rights and the increasing evidence of abuses, this option had no defenders in the group of high-level decisionmakers in Washington.

A second option was to decide that Somoza's legitimacy was evaporating. In this case, the United States might press him to resign and give way to a moderate opposition group with US support and mediation. This would involve a relatively visible involvement of, if not "intervention" by, the United States in the politics of Nicaragua, and an explicit commitment to removing a head of state. In early 1978, the only advocates for this line of action were relatively low-level professional foreign service personnel in the Latin American bureau at State.

A third possibility involved continued pressure on Somoza to improve his human rights record, but restraint in trying to influence internal Nicaraguan political matters. The United States would not press Somoza to leave, but rather urge him to reform. It would exercise pressure by means of manipulating military and economic aid, and it would avoid any direct involvement in mediation between Somoza and the opposition. This, by the generally accepted rules of the game, would avoid the risk of being charged (by Latin Americans as well as the US public) with intervening. This strategy assumed that Somoza could successfully resist revolutionary overthrow: It concerned itself not with the character of a new government, but with the behavior of the existing regime.

Such was the preferred approach of many advisers in Congress, the staff of the National Security Council, the State Department and the "human rights lobby." They wished to continue the moral stand on rights but, after the debacle of Vietnam and revelations concerning American involvement in Chilean politics in the 1970s, felt that "Carter should not overthrow a government . . . it was time to get out of the business, regardless of what the circumstances were."[21]

Nobody with official status in the United States was advocating tolerance or acceptance of a revolutionary government. The orthodox view was that dramatic social and economic change was necessary in Nicaragua to overcome inequalities of income, to raise the very low standards of public health and education, and to create a more just society. But only people outside of government drew the conclusion that a revolutionary structural change was necessary. Many Latin American and US intellectuals were in fact arguing that reforms could not do the job. Not only Somoza, but much of the system resulting from the dominance of private entrepreneur-led development would have to be changed.

But given the anti-imperialist, socialist ideology of the Sandinistas and their history of sympathy with Cuba, supporting the one group that was dedicated to such revolutionary change would have meant dealing with the possibility of strong Cuban (and potentially Soviet) affinities on the part of a revolutionary government and, perhaps, of a Stalinist regime. For official Washington, it was taken for granted that a FSLN victory was to be avoided. From a practical point of view, in any case, in early 1978 the FSLN was still a relatively small group in the country, facing the strong military organization of the National Guard.

EXERCISES

With the roles described above allocated to members of the class, each might be asked to give brief presentations to the group (as if at the February 15 meeting), covering the following questions:

1. *How serious is the crisis in Nicaragua, and in what way does it threaten or affect American interests in the region and more widely?*
2. *What should the objectives of US policy be?*
3. *What courses of action would best and least serve these objectives? What are the probable costs and benefits of each course of action?*

4. *What strategy would you recommend? What problems do you anticipate in implementing this strategy? How would you deal with these problems?*
5. *Is* negotiation *appropriate at this point? If so, who should be involved; what should the agenda be; what objects should the United States (if involved) seek through negotiation; and how should negotiation be conducted?*

NEGOTIATING THE SUCCESSION

The officials brought together in February 1978 by Christopher from State, the NSC, the CIA, and the joint chiefs decided on a policy involving continuing pressure for reforms and neutrality on domestic Nicaraguan politics. Somoza was felt to be strong enough to hold out, so that the tougher questions about succession did not come up. The Carter administration was preoccupied with the process of securing congressional approval of the Panama Canal treaties. In March 1978, the treaties were making their way through Congress with bare majorities secured by intense presidential lobbying. Pressing for an end to censorship, freeing political prisoners, and promises of honest elections satisfied the human rights lobby without seriously upsetting Somoza's friends in Congress, some of whom had key roles on committees which had to approve various aspects of the treaties.

President Carter wrote a letter responding to Venezuelan president Carlos Andres Perez's request for action, saying in part, "We can and will voice our preference for increased democratization. . . . But we will not intervene or impose specific political solutions for individual countries."[22]

Ambassador Solaun was instructed to urge Somoza to invite the Inter-American Human Rights Commission to Nicaragua. Approvals for new aid projects were temporarily frozen. Apparently without explicit instructions from Washington, Solaun also recommended to Somoza a public announcement that he would leave public office after the next elections in 1981, something that he was constitutionally required to do. The ambassador also suggested to opposition leaders that greater unity would make them more effective. But no more active role was taken, and somewhat later two more economic aid packages were approved, partly as the result of lobbying by Rep. Charles Wilson.

Somoza was eager for US support. On February 27, he gathered 100,000 supporters at an outdoor meeting and, speaking from a bulletproof enclosure, announced that he would retire from politics after the 1981 elections. After several months delay, he spoke of a package of reforms aimed at satisfying the critics on human rights. On June 19, he announced steps to free some political prisoners, declared that *Los Doce*, the exile group of opposition leaders, could return to Nicaragua, promised electoral reforms and promised to invite the Human Rights Commission of the OAS to Nicaragua to make an inspection. He followed this with a trip to the United States, lobbying for support, although he did not succeed in meeting with any high-level government officials.

On June 30, Somoza was rewarded with a letter from President Carter applauding the steps he had taken and urging him to continue to work toward further human rights guarantees. The letter said, in part:

> Dear Mr. President:
> I read your statements to the press on June 19 with great interest and appreciation. The steps toward respecting human rights that you are considering are important and heartening signs, and, as they are translated into actions, will mark a major advance for your nation in answering some of the criticisms recently aimed at the Nicaraguan government. . . .
> I look forward to hearing of the implementation of your decision and appreciate very much your announcement of these constructive actions. . . .[23]

The State Department asked that the letter be kept secret, apparently intending it as a prod to Somoza to fulfill his promises and not as a sign of support. But the existence of the letter and its general tone were soon public knowledge. Somoza himself used the letter in a meeting with Carlos Andres Perez to demonstrate Washington's support for him. It was widely understood as meaning that the United States was satisfied to let Somoza finish his term of office.

In Nicaragua, while these diplomatic maneuvers were going on, the largest alliance yet of anti-Somoza forces took shape. It was called the Broad Opposition Front (FAO). It included sixteen political, labor, and business organizations, and had good contacts with many others. The new front issued a manifesto calling for Somoza's departure, the formation of a national unity government to replace him and the reorganization of the National Guard to eliminate Somoza or any of his relatives from positions of command. The Sandinistas were linked to FAO through the membership of *Los Doce*. The FAO led the nonmilitary opposition throughout the latter half of 1978. To support its demands, the FAO called a general strike for late August.

By September, Somoza was under severe pressure. In late August, the FSLN staged another spectacular coup, taking over the National Palace while the Congress was in session and gaining both fame and money in return for releasing hostages taken on this occasion. Thousands of people turned out to cheer the guerrillas on their triumphant trip to the airport and exile. At the same time, the FAO-sponsored general strike and an apparently spontaneous uprising in the town of Matagalpa shook the country.

The Sandinistas followed up in early September with a series of attacks on National Guard positions throughout Nicaragua. It was now clear that the guerrillas had acquired a much broader base, bringing in many middle- and upper-class recruits as well as young people inspired by the events at the National Palace and in Matagalpa. The National Guard, giving no signs of disloyalty or doubts about Somoza, struck back with its accustomed ferocity. The conflict was becoming significantly more violent, and the society was becoming polarized.

Another level of escalation was added by the activities of Nicaragua's southern neighbors, who were moving to a more anti-Somoza position, and one more supportive of the armed opposition. In Costa Rica, a new president, Rodrigo Carazo, was elected in May 1978. After a period of formal neutrality toward the conflict in Nicaragua, Carazo became much more involved in the struggle against Somoza.[24] Venezuela's Carlos Andres Perez was also moving to more active support for the opposition.

In Washington, the National Palace attack, the FAO strike, and the September offensive of the FSLN coincided with delicate preparations for the Camp David meetings with Egypt and Israel, Carter's major foreign policy effort to bring peace to the Middle East. Nevertheless, the fighting brought Nicaragua more forcefully to the attention of US policymakers than ever before, prodded further by new letters from the presidents of Venezuela and Costa Rica asking for stronger US action. Another interagency policy group was formed, although in this period it was chaired by Brzezinski at the National Security Council. The human rights office in the State Department, in contrast to the earlier period, was much less prominent.

Another significant change in the cast of characters among the policy-makers was the emergence of a stronger voice from the ranks of the State Department professionals. By the end of August Ambassador Viron P. Vaky was taking a more active role in policymaking as the new assistant secretary of state for inter-American affairs. Vaky had been on the NSC staff under Kissinger, but most recently had been ambassador to Venezuela. On taking responsibility for Latin American policy at the State Department, he made it clear that he favored the use of American pressure to bring about a "gradual opening" of political life in the Central American states, without destroying the armed forces or directly challenging the enrichment of incumbent dictators.

To reformulate policy, Vaky instigated a series of interagency meetings that began on August 29 (even before the major FSLN offensive had been launched). In view of the worsening situation and initiatives from Costa Rica and Venezuela, a consensus emerged on a more active posture seeking to influence the outcomes of the conflict between Somoza and the opposition. The question became how to act, and with what goals.

At a meeting on September 4, under secretary of state David Newsom set out a general premise that all present accepted, namely, "that, ultimately, Somoza had to go. The question was how."[25] Vaky, supported by leading officials in the State Department, pressed again for a direct approach to Somoza (to urge him to resign). He also wanted negotiations with the opposition leading to a new government. By this time, the line officers at State had concluded that the main goal should be Somoza's departure.

On the other side, Robert Pastor (the NSC adviser on Latin America) and Anthony Lake (director of policy planning at the State Department) argued that the United States should not be seen to be taking the lead in engineering the removal of a foreign head of state. They found themselves on the same side as Brzezinski and representatives of the Defense Department who felt that Somoza and the National Guard still represented the best bulwark against a leftist takeover. This group felt that steps to force the Somozas out should not be taken until an alternative was in place.

Congress continued to be a channel for pressure, but in more than one direction. Representatives Murphy and Wilson composed a letter to Carter with the signatures of seventy-six of their colleagues, warning of the possibility of another Cuba and asking for support for Somoza. In response, Representative Donald Frazer (D-MN) answered with another letter, with eighty-six signatures, asking for Somoza's resignation. Key votes on the Panama Canal treaties were still due.

The leadership at State and the NSC, supported by the majority of the political appointees in the process, including Pastor and Lake, were still reluctant to move directly into the Nicaraguan political situation. Their caution derived from the president's public commitment to the principles of nonintervention and from fear of adverse public reaction both in the United States and in Latin America. Although they agreed on the necessity of a more active role, they sought some formula that would reduce the exposure of the United States. Rather than a direct approach to Somoza, they favored playing a mediating role between Somoza and the opposition.

Mediation, September-December 1978

Nicaragua's neighbors (even Venezuela and Costa Rica) were not enthusiastic about being involved in mediation between Somoza and his enemies, preferring that the United States take the lead. Somoza himself was contemptuous of plans for outside involvement. On September 1, he declared that American foreign policy had fallen into "the hands of leftists and Communists." Five days later, he told Solaun that his government "would neither request nor tolerate OAS intervention." Washington, he asserted, was being duped by Venezuela. Moreover, the United States was encouraging the foolish ambitions of some Nicaraguans: "Because of your human rights policy [Somoza declared], a bunch of imbeciles [in Nicaragua] have thought that you are going to overthrow me. Do not contribute more to the tragedy of this country."[26] As for suggestions that foreigners be brought in to monitor elections, Somoza considered them naive: "Latins," he declared, "don't know how to compromise and don't understand free elections."

The Nicaraguan opposition (apart from the FSLN) seemed to favor mediation. On September 3 Solaun reported a meeting with business leaders in Managua and another with Archbishop Obando y Bravo: "All of them [he said] had urged mediation by the United States."

Both in the United States and in Central America, matters came to a head on September 12. At an interagency meeting in Washington, Vaky and Under Secretary Newsom argued that the United States had to take on the role of mediator, but Christopher, Lake, Pastor, and others wanted the initiative left to the Central Americans. Eventually, it was decided to send Ambassador William J. Jorden to Central America to consult regional heads of state. Jorden was also to meet FAO leaders in Managua and suggest that their organization appeal for international mediation. President Carter, then embroiled in the Camp David negotiations, accepted the proposal for mediation, describing it as "one of the most difficult tasks which we have ever undertaken."[27]

Jorden found on traveling to Central America that there was little enthusiasm within or outside Nicaragua for becoming involved in an effort to solve the conflict by mediation.[28] Somoza made his work harder by choosing to bomb Costa Rica, causing Carazo to withdraw as a prospective mediator.

Neither side within Nicaragua seemed attracted to mediation. Though Solaun had persuaded the FAO to appeal to the OAS for mediation, another official noted: "The FAO didn't want mediation. Neither did Tacho." Referring to the repression of the Matagalpa rising, one member of the FAO declared: "A river of blood separates us. How can we sit down and negotiate with a man who has just slaughtered three thousand Nicaraguans?"[29]

On September 21, Panama warned Washington that Venezuelan planes were about to attack Managua (using Panamanian bases). This threat pushed the doubters in the Carter administration into agreeing to United States participation in mediation. Faced with a regional conflict, Brzezinski even told the Panamanians that the US would be prepared to consider action affecting the composition of governments in the region "if it were a genuine collective effort." In other words, Washington was now prepared to contemplate pressing Somoza to resign.

Despite this tougher attitude, officials in Washington were still divided over strategy. The general hope was that the mediation would find a formula by which Somoza would leave and the moderate opposition would form a new government. Some officials believed that the United States should admit that its goal was to remove Somoza while there was a moderate center that could take over; with this goal in mind, policymakers could decide ahead of time on a strategy to achieve that end.

Other officials preferred not to make such hard decisions immediately, but to "play it by ear" and act in terms of the context of the circumstances at the time. They were, in fact, stalling in the hope that the Nicaraguans would remove Somoza by themselves. Brzezinski feared that the United States would be blamed if intervention failed to establish a moderate government. Looking at the loose coalition of sixteen parties in opposition, he wondered if they could form such a government: If they didn't, the FSLN might well move into the vacuum.

The more aggressive American attitude toward Somoza was conveyed to him at a meeting with Jorden on September 23. Jorden made it clear to the dictator that, in the US view, he was the major cause of the problem faced by Nicaragua. For the first time, a US representative gingerly suggested to the embattled president that "the possibility of your departure from office before 1981 is one of the possibilities that has to be considered."[30] Somoza rejected the idea of resignation, announcing that he intended to stay in office until 1981.

On the same day, the OAS foreign ministers met and showed themselves wary of anything that might seem to endorse or even imply intervention. They approved a resolution authorizing "conciliation efforts" in the Nicaraguan conflict (to placate Somoza the term *conciliation* was buried in a sonorous title--"The OAS Sponsored Commission on Friendly Cooperation and Conciliation").

After much haggling about which countries should be involved, it was decided that Guatemala and the Dominican Republic would join the United States in the mediation and that the American representative would be

William P. Bowdler, a diplomat with substantial Latin American experience and currently director of the Bureau of Intelligence and Research in the State Department.

In the negotiations that followed, the FAO spoke for the opposition. Somoza negotiated for himself, although occasionally he spoke through the leadership of the official Nationalist Liberal party. Bowdler was empowered by Washington to seek arrangements for a transfer of power, the successor government to Somoza to be based on free elections. Originally, Bowdler's instructions stated that the United States might seek Somoza's departure "substantially in advance of 1981"; at the insistence of Christopher, the word "substantially" was deleted.

The situation that the mediators found in Nicaragua was discouraging. The fighting in September had deepened the hostility between the two sides; it had also given each confidence that it could win without negotiation. Neither was interested in communicating through an intermediary except to get the other to surrender. Somoza himself seemed oblivious to the anger that the mediators found among the general population in and outside Managua. An American journalist noted: "Confined to the Bunker, Somoza seemed to have lost touch with reality and acted more like a businessman negotiating real estate than a chief of state upon whose decisions the life of a nation depended. While he continued to rant and rave and humiliate those around him, even during the negotiation sessions, he was showing signs of tension. His facial tic and shaky hand grew more pronounced."[31]

In these circumstances, the mediators decided not to try to press the parties to negotiate directly but rather to encourage them to set down their demands formally. Neither was willing to do so: Both seemed to want to use the mediators (and particularly Bowdler) as a deus ex machina to get rid of the other.[32] The FAO was overwhelmingly concerned with speeding Somoza's departure. The dictator's response was "reminiscent of a last-ditch stand in a second-rate gangster film: 'If they want me,' he said, 'they'd better come in and get me.'"[33] Even before the mediating team arrived, he announced plans to double the size of the National Guard and had undertaken an aggressive arms-purchasing campaign.

The first proposal of the mediating team was for Somoza to resign with the formation of an interim government that would prepare for elections in 1981. To form that government, it proposed negotiations between the FAO and Somoza's Nationalist Liberal party. The National Guard would be reorganized. As a means of pressure, the United States slowed down aid and convinced the International Monetary Fund (IMF) to delay a substantial standby loan.

The FAO reacted negatively. It rejected the idea of allowing the new government to depend on negotiations with Somoza's party. After considerable internal debate, it put forward an alternative proposal that Somoza resign immediately and that the interim government be made up of two representatives of Somoza's party and two each of the sixteen organizations making up the FAO. It accepted the continued existence of the National Guard, as long as none of Somoza's relatives was an officer.[34] Under this proposal, a constitutional assembly would prepare the country for elections in December 1981.

In reaching this position, however, the consensus in the FAO broke down. One of its negotiators (a man with ties to the FSLN) resigned and *Los Doce* left the FAO, complaining that Somoza was being allowed too much influence in the proposed successor government.

The loss of *Los Doce* was significant because they were the only strong link between the FAO and the Sandinistas. Their departure meant that the FAO no longer had any organized military force. Some observers believed that the Sandinistas themselves had dictated Ramirez's resignation, finding diplomatic justification for a tactical action determined by their own interests. In this view, they needed a battlefield victory. Mediation, on the contrary, threatened to bring about a negotiated outcome in which the more moderate FAO would succeed Somoza.[35]

Somoza was encouraged by the fragmentation of the opposition. He now asserted that it would be unconstitutional for him to give up his office before the end of his term in 1981. If he were to leave, he claimed, the FAO would be faced with dealing with the Sandinistas and without a strong National Guard to defend themselves. Instead, Somoza proposed a plebiscite, which would lead to one of two outcomes. If the FAO won, it would be allowed to share power with him until 1981; if he won, he would continue in office alone and the FAO would be required to support him. The FAO, predictably, rejected this idea as "completely absurd."

DISCUSSION QUESTIONS

1. *What does the course of the negotiations up to this point suggest to you about the appropriateness of negotiation as a way of solving this dispute? What alternatives to negotiation were available? What would have been the costs and benefits of each?*
2. *In particular, was mediation the most appropriate form of negotiation? What problems and advantages did it offer?*

3. *How did the use of mediation strengthen the hands of some parties and weaken those of others?*
4. *What merits and flaws do you see in the initial proposal put to Somoza?*
5. *What evidence can you glean about both the aims of those involved and their expectations from the negotiation?*
6. *How do you evaluate US policy regarding the mediation, first, in relation to prevailing US objectives and, secondly, in relation to your view of American interests in Nicaragua?*

The Failure of Mediation

Convinced that Somoza's resignation was now the minimal condition for a peaceful solution, Bowdler returned to Washington and joined Vaky in pressing for sanctions against the dictator. They wanted immediate application of sanctions against Somoza in order to bring about his departure from office. But Christopher and Brzezinski "demurred," preferring to threaten Somoza with sanctions (notably US blocking of a Nicaraguan application for IMF credit) unless he accepted the FAO's latest proposal. It was agreed to tell Somoza of the American intention to block the IMF application and to cut further bilateral aid to Nicaragua. But two more meetings with Somoza produced only further rejections and repetition of his idea of a plebiscite. By this time, the FAO was becoming impatient with the mediators: It gave Somoza until November 21 to leave Nicaragua, failing which it would withdraw from the process.

At meetings in Washington on November 12 and 13, Bowdler suggested that Somoza had been shaken by the American threat of sanctions and argued for even greater pressure. Bowdler dismissed the plebiscite idea as "a stalling tactic," intended to stretch out the negotiations. Vaky agreed, commenting: "He's throwing sand in our faces." Both men urged that the United States should force Somoza out before the moderate opposition collapsed, to the benefit of the Sandinistas.

Pastor and Oxman (special assistant to Christopher) said that the United States could not be seen to reject something that looked like an election (especially given the activism of Somoza's friends in Congress). The plebiscite, they thought, should be turned into a vote on Somoza's staying in power. In such a form, it would give new legitimacy to the mediation process and would force the FAO to come together as united party. "We felt," Pastor reportedly said, "that the US should not intervene militarily or even politically in the sense of promoting the overthrow of Somoza. The Carter administration constrained itself by its belief that it was inappropriate for the US in the future, in part because it's been so usual in the past, to overthrow governments. On the other hand, we felt that assistance, whether economic or military, whether bilateral or multilateral, was an appropriate instrument to influence developments."[36]

Vaky and Bowdler were unconvinced by Pastor's strategy, believing that Somoza would create a new issue out of the procedure for the plebiscite. They warned that if the FAO rejected the plebiscite, however altered, and Somoza accepted it, "Washington would be left on Somoza's side of the question with no place to go. And if the negotiations simply dragged on, with a new outbreak of fighting, the Sandinistas would gain at the expense of the moderates in the FAO as well as of Somoza."[37] Brzezinski questioned the diplomats' belief that Somoza could be forced out. Bowdler admitted that the chances of the dictator resigning were "a little better than fifty-fifty." If he didn't, Brzezinski protested, then "Washington could easily end up embarrassed and without leverage in a deteriorating situation." He and Vance overruled the professional foreign service officers again and sided with Pastor and Oxman. Vaky considered resignation at this point, but both he and Bowdler decided to persist. When Bowdler returned to Managua, he found that Representatives Murphy and Wilson had preceded him and were advising Somoza (in the latter's words) "to stick around" and not to give in to "the goddamned commies, here and there."[38]

The mediation panel revised the plebiscite idea so that its purpose would be "to consult the Nicaraguan people on whether or not the President of the Republic should remain in office."[39] The voting would be subject to international supervision and would occur only after Somoza lifted the state of siege currently in force. If Somoza lost, he would leave the country and the FAO's plan for a transitional government would take effect. If he won, the Somoza plan for limited power-sharing would take effect. Reluctantly, the FAO accepted the plan, on condition that Somoza leave the country during the voting. It then announced that it would not take part in any further talks, arguing that it had already been maneuvered into a huge retreat from principle by even agreeing to an election in which Somoza would compete. Somoza, for his part, rejected the proposal, objecting to the provision for international supervision.

In further haggling, Somoza was careful not to reject the idea of a plebiscite altogether: Such rejection would give the United States a chance to abandon *him* altogether. Meanwhile, Washington's problems were complicated by the activities of Wilson and other friends of Somoza who threatened to withdraw support for ratification of the Panama Canal treaty unless the Carter administration support Somoza and the "anti-Communist struggle" in Central America. The State Department, Wilson claimed, was being run by a "bunch of adolescent anarchists."[40]

The FAO reluctantly went along with minor changes in the plebiscite plan, but it was clear that the main negotiations at this time were taking place between the US-dominated mediation panel and Somoza. The Americans were not at this time actively pursuing separate negotiations with the FAO, with a view to its assuming power as a third-force government. Indeed, the political position of the FAO was distinctly perilous: Four of its member groups had resigned and the Sandinistas (now united) were loud in their denunciation of "the imperialist mediation."[41]

Nevertheless, the Carter administration was increasingly optimistic about the possibility of a plebiscite, especially since both sides had agreed (for the first time) to direct, face-to-face talks. At these meetings, the FAO insisted that if Somoza lost, he must leave the country, with its transitional plan then taking effect. If he won, it would remain in nonviolent opposition "but would not participate in the government." On both points, the FAO was supported by the mediators, who nevertheless also insisted that, in the event of a victory, Somoza must be allowed to reorganize his government as he saw fit. Somoza's representatives objected to the FAO's refusal to agree to participate in a prospective "government of reconciliation," as well as to its demand that Somoza leave Nicaragua if he lost.

While these talks were underway, Somoza indirectly approached Bowdler to ask whether, if he left Nicaragua, the United States would grant him asylum and would guarantee both that his assets would be left alone and that he would be protected against extradition. Washington sent an essentially legal answer to the effect that asylum would be granted, but that the other guarantees could not be offered unconditionally.[42]

At the next meeting of the two sides on December 20, Somoza's party suddenly began to behave "in an inconsiderate manner," disrupting the mediators' presentation of their draft proposal on the plebiscite.[43] The meeting was adjourned and Bowdler, normally a discreet and controlled person, finally lost patience with Somoza's delegation.

The meaning of the events of December 20 was not immediately clear, but the United States decided to apply direct pressure to Somoza from someone it thought he would take seriously. On December 21, General Dennis McAuliffe, head of the US Southern Command, flew from Panama to Managua and, accompanied by Bowdler, tried to talk Somoza into leaving. Somoza recalled that Bowdler "began making the same old pitch and complaining about a lack of cooperation."[44] McAuliffe then spoke to Somoza: "The reason that I'm here is that we perceive that the cooperation you have given to the negotiating team is no longer evident. . . . We on the military side of the US recognize . . . that peace will not come to Nicaragua until you have removed yourself from the presidency and the scene."[45] Somoza refused to resign, adding that as far as the plebiscite was concerned, there would be no problem so long as it was organized along "traditional lines" (a reassurance the opposition would have found ominous).

Bowdler concluded that the mediation process "had hit a wall" and at an interagency meeting on December 26 it was decided to stop efforts to find a solution and to impose limited sanctions on Somoza. No further progress was made in talks in Managua, and on January 12 US policymakers met and concluded that Somoza was stalling. They warned him that the United States was about to reassess its relations with Nicaragua, but the dictator only responded by attacking the mediators' proposals and repeating his existing December proposals.

On January 19, the FAO announced that the negotiations were over, and on February 1 the United States formally ended its military assistance to Nicaragua. It also announced that no new economic assistance would be forthcoming (without stopping aid in the pipeline) and withdrew Peace Corps volunteers and about half of its Embassy personnel.[46] Somoza took the sanctions in his stride and said that "things would go on as before."[47] The United States did not withdraw recognition, but Ambassador Solaun returned to Washington.

For the next five and a half crucial months, the United States had neither ambassador nor special envoys in Managua. No new initiatives were undertaken.

DISCUSSION QUESTIONS

1. *To what extent (and for whom) was the mediation effort a failure? Why did it fail?*
2. *What did the mediation reveal about the power of particular parties to the negotiation, their stakes in a negotiated solution, and their reasons for being involved in it?*
3. *What, if any, tactical changes might have improved the chances of the mediation's succeeding?*
4. *How did the outcome of the mediation alter the relationship between the United States and Somoza? In retrospect, does it seem to you that the*

United States was wise to have suggested mediation? What other policy or procedure might have worked better?

5. *To what extent did the outcome of the mediation serve Somoza's interests? How did it strengthen or weaken the opposition's position?*

NEGOTIATING THE SUCCESSION: ENDGAME

By June 1979, the struggle between Somoza and his opponents had become almost entirely military in character. With the collapse of the mediation effort, the FAO ceased to be politically significant and the initiative passed to the FSLN.

Through an organization called the United People's Movement (MPU), the Sandinistas had begun to create neighborhood committees. In March 1979, the FSLN finally created a joint military command with a pact signed in Cuba.

Nicaragua's neighbors sided more and more openly with the opposition. In May, Mexico actually broke off diplomatic relations with Nicaragua, but (perhaps because of US pressure) no other Central American country followed suit. The United States urged Costa Rica and Panama not to supply arms to the FSLN, and in fact these countries, along with Venezuela, pursued a complex diplomacy--trying to bring down Somoza without allowing an expansion of Cuban influence onto the mainland or offending the United States. Costa Rica and Panama worked to increase the influence of one leader, Eden Pastora, within the guerrilla movement since they believed him to be the most pragmatic of the FSLN's leaders.

By June, the Sandinistas were undertaking their final offensive. A force moved across the border from Costa Rica, a smaller group moved in from Honduras, and uprisings were taking place in many of the major cities and towns. Somoza tried and failed to get an OAS condemnation of Costa Rica for allowing the invasion. In the south, the National Guard and the Sandinistas fought their first regular battles, as opposed to the hit-and-run attacks of guerrilla war. The National Guard still showed no sign of weakening its loyalty to Somoza, and the fighting was bitter.

On June 16, a provisional governing junta was formed in Costa Rica by the rebels. Of the five members, three were closely associated with the Sandinistas: the other two were Chamorro's widow, Violeta, and Alfonso Robelo, the business leader and former negotiator for the FAO.

Other Latin American countries were publicly turning more and more against Somoza. On June 16, the Andean countries declared that they recognized a "state of belligerency" in Nicaragua, giving the rebels equal status with Somoza.

Prior to June, the CIA and the US Embassy in Managua had been confident that the National Guard could prevail over the guerrillas. At a meeting on January 26, CIA director Stansfield Turner had predicted that Somoza would be able to hold on to power until 1981. In the first half of the year, Somoza had a very large stockpile of arms and was able to defeat the US blockade through sources in Israel and, later, Guatemala and El Salvador. On June 12, however, the CIA shifted its evaluation and concluded that Somoza's overthrow was a matter of weeks away.[48] Intelligence sources were also reporting increased arms flows from Cuba. The possibility of a Sandinista victory had become very real. There was no disagreement among the top policymakers in Washington that a FSLN victory would be bad for the United States.

At meetings at the NSC in June, a variety of options were debated. Up to this time, the United States had worked for keeping a (reformed) National Guard as the defense against a complete takeover by the guerrilla forces. The growing success of the final offensive led policymakers to conclude that only external forces would make that possible. Brzezinski briefly argued for US military intervention, but the idea was rejected. The policy of working through the OAS was reaffirmed, and again, with the support of Brzezinski in particular, it was decided to press for an inter-American peacekeeping force that would enter Nicaragua to enforce a ceasefire and install an interim government.

At the OAS, Vance for the first time publicly suggested Somoza's resignation, and on June 23, the OAS voted to approve a resolution calling for Somoza to step down from office (only Nicaragua and Paraguay voting against). But despite growing worries about the Sandinistas, Latin Americans were not ready for the sharp departure that the intervention of a multinational army would represent. Sympathy for the Sandinistas, hope that they would abide by their promises of a broadly-based ruling group and reluctance to sanction what would undoubtedly be a predominantly US force combined to frustrate this last-minute effort by the United States to reverse the course of events. The OAS voted decisively against the resolution to create a peacekeeping force.

The policy community in Washington appeared to be roughly divided into two factions. The first, centering on the NSC, was preoccupied with the military dimensions and, specifically, with trying to forestall a Sandinista military victory. Once the idea of unilateral intervention and an inter-American peacekeeping force was rejected, this group concentrated on rebuilding the National Guard so that it could retain some legitimacy after the overthrow. Several efforts were made to contact a former National Guard leader who had been eased out by Somoza and was presently serving the Nicaraguan government abroad.

The group centered in the State Department, on the other hand, was concentrating on the next government. Its aim was to influence the incoming junta and, in particular, to expand its representation so as to minimize Sandinista domination. Ambassador Bowdler was sent to San Jose in Costa Rica to meet with the junta. Supported by the recently out-of-office (but still active) Venezuelan ex-president, Carlos Andres Perez, Bowdler tried to persuade the junta's members to include among their number a majority of non-FSLN members. They ran into opposition not only from the FSLN, but also from Violeta Chamorro, who considered them to be interfering in Nicaraguan affairs.

Meanwhile, the offensive rolled on, with the rebels taking several key towns. Popular enthusiasm for the revolution was growing, and many Nicaraguans joined in the final assaults. The bloodiest fighting was in the south where Somoza threw his strongest forces against the FSLN's main thrust, managing to stall the offensive in that area. Eden Pastora, the regional rebel commander, sent a message to the White House through the ex-president of Costa Rica, Jose Figueres, suggesting that the United States get Somoza to pull his forces away from the southern front so that he, Pastora, could arrive in Managua first. This would ensure that the least Marxist and least pro-Cuban wing of the FSLN would have the most important role in the subsequent government. The United States turned down the suggestion, apparently because they still hoped that a military stalemate would develop between the FSLN and the National Guard, making a negotiated solution possible.[49]

In Managua, the new US ambassador, Lawrence Pezzullo, negotiated with Somoza, urging his resignation and trying to get an acceptable transition formula. On July 6, with fighting already going on in the capital, Somoza finally bent to US pressure and announced that he would resign as soon as the United States told him to do so. Pezzullo's efforts then centered on forging an interim government based on the constitutionally appropriate leaders of the Nicaraguan Congress. This group, it was hoped, would make the transition to the junta, trying to ensure the survival of the National Guard as a military force to balance the guerrilla army.

The junta (in large part to placate US worries) agreed on July 11 to integrate all National Guardsmen into the new army if they immediately abandoned their weapons when Somoza resigned. It also issued a statement promising free elections.

Three days later, the junta announced a cabinet, including only one member identified as a fully committed Sandinista, Tomas Borge of the Proletarian faction (named interior minister). Although that position was obviously a key one, the minimal role of the Sandinistas in this publicly declared version of the new government was clearly meant as a conciliatory move.

On July 17, Pezzullo had Somoza appoint a new head of the National Guard, purge almost all of the older members of the Guard, and agree to turn over power to the president of the Chamber of Deputies, Francisco Urcuyo. Urcuyo was then to turn over power to the junta and merge the National Guard, under new leadership, with the guerrilla forces. Somoza boarded a plane and went into exile in his luxurious house in Miami.

This final arrangement by the United States fell apart. The junta had never promised to negotiate with Urcuyo nor to integrate the National Guard *as a unit*. Further, in a final tragi-comical stroke, Urcuyo decided that he would refuse to turn over power to "the Communists." In the day or two of indecision that resulted, the National Guard simply dissolved. Many fled the country, some taking what they could across the border into neighboring countries, others further away. The Sandinistas ceased negotiations and demanded unconditional surrender from the remainder of Somoza's regime. Urcuyo and the new head of the National Guard fled to Guatemala. The revolutionary army, swollen by thousands of volunteers, swept into the capital.

The way was clear for the triumphal entry of the junta and the FSLN's National Directorate into Managua on July 20, 1979. Things had not worked out the way that US policymakers had hoped.

DISCUSSION QUESTIONS

1. *What options were open to the US government during the last phase of the crisis? How feasible and appropriate was each?*
2. *What, in your view, should have been the objectives of the US government in the last phase of the crisis? How might it have tried to achieve these objectives?*
3. *Would negotiation have been possible at any point in this last phase? If so, between whom and around what agenda should it have been attempted?*

4. *Was a Sandinista victory "inevitable"? If not, how did the actions or inactions of the US government and Somoza, respectively, make it more or less likely?*
5. *Was the notion of a transfer of power to the constitutional liberals and conservatives an illusion? What were the limits on US capacity to bring about such a transfer?*

NOTES

1. The text for this section is adapted from Alex R. Hybel, *The United States and Nicaragua: Anatomy of a Failed Negotiation for Regime Change, 1977-1979* (Pew case study no. 327), 1.

2. *Ibid.*, 2.

3. *Ibid.*

4. *Ibid.*, 3.

5. *Ibid.*

6. Shirley Christian, *Nicaragua. Revolution in the Family* (New York: Vintage Books, 1986), 29.

7. *Ibid.*, 3-4.

8. *Ibid.*

9. *Ibid.*, 5.

10. Bernard Diederich, *Somoza and the Legacy of U.S. Involvement in Central America* (New York: E. P. Dutton, 1981), 125.

11. Anthony Lake, *Somoza Falling. The Nicaraguan Dilemma: A Portrait of Washington at Work* (Boston: Houghton Mifflin, 1989), 14.

12. From 1950 to 1970 the United States provided more than $30 million of such aid and provided training for 5,670 Nicaraguan officers, much of it under the anti-insurgency programs started by the Kennedy administration. Economic aid to Nicaragua was larger. Between 1962 and 1977 Nicaragua received about $212 million. It was less directly in support of Somoza, since it also helped entrepreneurs who became Somoza's opposition, but Somoza was able to profit directly and indirectly.

13. Christian, *Nicaragua*, 10.

14. For his efforts, Cheek was later honored by the American Foreign Service Association.

15. See Robert A. Pastor, *Condemned to Repetition: The United States and Nicaragua* (Princeton, NJ: Princeton University Press, 1987), 38.

16. Anastasio Somoza Debayle, *Nicaragua Betrayed* (Belmont, MA: Western Islands, 1980), 58.

17. Christian, *Nicaragua*, 42.

18. *Ibid.*, 41.

19. The text for this section is adapted from Hybel, *The United States and Nicaragua*, 13.

20. *Ibid.*, 52.

21. Pastor, quoted in *Ibid.*, 76.

22. Pastor, *Condemned*, 63.

23. Cited in Douglas Chalmers, *Nicaragua, 1978-1979: The United States and Anastasio Somoza. Dealing with Friendly Dictators Who Are Losing Their Authority* (Pew case no. 105), 28.

24. "Formal" because Carazo in fact tolerated active help for the Nicaraguan rebels by Costa Rican sympathizers.

25. Lake, *Somoza Falling*, 135.

26. *Ibid.*, 137.

27. Diederich, *Somoza*, 205.

28. Rachel McCleary, *The Ethics of Intervention: The United States and Nicaragua* (Pew case no. 347), 5.

29. Diederich, *Somoza*, 205.

30. Somoza, *Nicaragua Betrayed*, 318.

31. Diederich, *Somoza*, 208. The Bunker was Somoza's headquarters outside the capital.

32. Lake notes: "Each faction seemed to see in Bowdler's presence a return to the old American deus ex machina that could be made to serve its own political interests while confounding those of its enemies" (*Somoza Falling*, 147).

33. Diederich, *Somoza*, 208.

34. Somoza's son, Tachito, was a major in the National Guard and director of the Basic Infantry Training School.

35. See Diederich, *Somoza*, 209; Lake, *Somoza Falling*, 148; McCleary, *Ethics of Intervention*, 7.

36. Quoted in Hybel, *The United States and Nicaragua*, 22.

37. Lake, *Somoza Falling*, 156.

38. Diederich, *Somoza*, 213.

39. United States, Department of State, *Report to the Secretary of State on the Work of the International Commission of Friendly Cooperation and Conciliation for Achieving a Peaceful Solution to the Grave Crisis of the Republic of Nicaragua*, July 1979, 10.

40. Diederich, *Somoza*, 225.

41. Lake, *Somoza Falling*, 159-160.

42. *Ibid.*, 159-160. Lake notes that the question was treated as purely legal and technical in content: the message containing it was not shown to Pastor.

43. United States, Department of State, *Report*, 13.

44. Diederich, *Somoza*, 223. Somoza told an aide that he was disappointed when he saw that Bowdler was with the general: "I knew then it would be the same old crap," he remarked.

45. Lake, *Somoza Falling*, 163.

46. Military assistance had been suspended in September 1978.

47. Chalmers, *Nicaragua, 1978-1979*, 37.

48. Pastor, *Condemned to Repetition*, 130.

49. Christian, *Nicaragua*, 105.

FURTHER READING ON NICARAGUA

Books

Booth, John A. *The End and the Beginning: The Nicaraguan Revolution*. Boulder, CO: Westview Press, 1982.

Christian, Shirley. *Nicaragua. Revolution in the Family*. New York: Vintage Books, 1986.

Diederich, Bernard. *Somoza and the Legacy of US Involvement in Central America*. New York: E. P. Dutton, 1981.

Kamman, William. *A Search for Stability: United States Diplomacy Toward Nicaragua 1925-1933*. Notre Dame, IN: University of Notre Dame Press, 1968.

LaFeber, Walter. *Inevitable Revolutions*. New York: W. W. Norton, 1984.

Lake, Anthony. *Somoza Falling. The Nicaraguan Dilemma: A Portrait of Washington at Work*. Boston: Houghton Mifflin, 1989.

Millett, Richard. *Guardians of the Dynasty*. Maryknoll, NY: Orbis, 1977.

Pastor, Robert A. *Condemned to Repetition: The United States and Nicaragua*. Princeton, NJ: Princeton University Press, 1987.

Schoultz, Lars. *National Security and United States Policy Toward Latin America*. Princeton, NJ: Princeton University Press, 1987.

Somoza Debayle, Anastasio (as told to Jack Cox). *Nicaragua Betrayed*. Belmont, MA: Western Islands, 1980.

4

IRAN, 1978–1979
The Fall of the Shah

The fall of the shah of Iran in 1978-1979 offers a chance to compare the handling of two crises by the same administration--that of President Jimmy Carter. We see some of the same characters as in the Nicaraguan case, and we see issues framed in a similar fashion. But the setting and the significance of the crises were very different. Iran was both more distant from the United States than Nicaragua and of substantially greater geopolitical significance (at least for Carter's foreign policy advisers). It was a large, wealthy, and powerful state, situated close to the Soviet Union, in a region controlling important oil reserves and afflicted by endemic, violent conflict. The regime itself appeared to be more sophisticated and dominant than the Latin American dictatorships; it also seemed more capable than they were of dealing with the United States on equal terms and was regarded with a respect sometimes approaching awe by US officials.

The forces opposing the regime were also different, both in sheer numbers and in disposition. Unlike the (by now) familiar Marxist liberation movements, the religious fundamentalists led by Khomeini were, for US policymakers, a new and startling phenomenon--one they initially underestimated and subsequently misunderstood.

This chapter is primarily the work of Gregory Treverton (with James Klocke) as presented in their case study, The Fall of the Shah of Iran, *Pew case study no. 311, with additional material inserted by the editor from Andrew Steigman,* The Iranian Hostage Negotiations, November 1979-January 1981 *(Pew case study no. 348) and from other cases and secondary sources as indicated in the notes.*

As in the earlier crises, the Iranian crisis led to an immediate, sustained, and angry argument about the conduct of American policymaking. This argument centered on some broader problems encountered in such crises. The case has been designed to illustrate several such problems, notably those of divided responsibility, ambiguous and incomplete intelligence, and conflicting views about the appropriate strategy to adopt. It particularly focuses on the dilemmas of the US ambassador--"the man on the spot"--and on the conflicts in Washington between the NSC and the State Department and between junior and senior officials.

*   *   *

In November 1977, an embarrassing incident occurred on the White House lawn. During the arrival ceremonies for the shah of Iran, police nearby fired tear gas canisters to stop fighting between rival groups of demonstrators--Iranian students numbering roughly sixty thousand who were intent on expressing either their hostility to or support for the shah. When the wind carried the tear gas over the ceremonies, the world was treated to the sight of President Carter, the shah and other senior officials wiping tears from their eyes. At a state dinner that night, Carter broke the tension by quipping: "There is one thing I can say about the shah: He knows how to draw a crowd." Carter went on to deliver lavish praise in a toast to Iranian-American relations.

THE STATUS QUO

Despite the extended history and intensity of Iranian-American relations, few Americans in the late 1970s knew much about Iran--or Persia, as it had been known prior to the 1930s. The United States had first focused seriously on Iran during World War II. Britain and the Soviet Union had occupied the country in 1941 to keep it out of German hands and had installed twenty-three-year-old Mohammed Reza Pahlavi on the throne in place of his father. At the Tehran Conference two years later, Franklin Roosevelt drew Winston Churchill and Joseph Stalin into a joint pledge to respect Iran's independence and territorial integrity when the war ended.[1]

It took renewed US involvement in 1945-1946 to make the Soviets honor their part of the bargain. American pressure, both directly and at the United Nations, was critical in persuading the Soviets to withdraw from the puppet state they had set up in their zone of occupation in northern Iran and thus in consolidating the young shah in power.[2]

When the next threat to the shah arose, the United States again played a key role in helping him maintain his rule. In a surge of nationalist fervor, the Iranian parliament in 1951 nationalized the British-owned Anglo-Iranian Oil Company. Britain responded with a worldwide boycott of Iranian oil, which served only to fuel the fires of Iranian nationalism. Over the ensuing two years, the shah found himself increasingly challenged by Mohammed Mossadegh, whom he had named prime minister but who was seeking to augment his own power at the shah's expense. As the struggle continued, Mossadegh's popular support began to slip, leaving him with the solid backing only from the Communist-led Tudeh party. The threat of renewed Soviet influence galvanized the United States into action, this time in the form of CIA backing for successful action by the armed forces to oust Mossadegh and restore the shah's authority.[3]

With the Mossadegh challenge behind him, the shah embarked in 1963 on his "White Revolution"--an ambitious program to transform his country both economically and militarily. In his mind, as he told the British ambassador, Iran "was part of Western civilisation, separated by an accident of geography from its natural partners and equals. The Iranians in his view were Aryan, not Semitic, and their innate talents and abilities had been suffocated by the blanket of the Arab invasion 1,200 years previously and its spiritual concomitant, Islam. He saw it as his mission to lift this blanket and to restore Iran to its former grandeur among the Great Powers."[4] Once again, the United States was to play a key role. The United States became the principal source of the technology needed to modernize the Iranian economy, of many of the ideas that underlay the Westernization of Iranian society, and of nearly all the weaponry essential to insuring that the Iranian armed forces could protect the country against external enemies and the shah against any further domestic threats. Fueled by the massive oil revenues of the late 1960s and early 1970s, the Iranian economy boomed, and prosperity (along with repression) silenced all but a handful of critics of the shah's authoritarian methods.[5]

After 1972, the US-Iranian relationship became even more special as President Richard Nixon and then Assistant for National Security Affairs Henry Kissinger cut a deal with the shah that had no counterpart in US relations with the Third World.[6] In effect, Nixon and Kissinger offered the shah carte blanche in buying American nonnuclear weaponry in exchange for a commitment to assume the role of Western policeman in the Persian Gulf region. With America reluctant to take on overseas commitments in the wake of the Vietnam experience, Nixon and Kissinger saw this as the best way to block Soviet influence in a vital area.[7]

Kissinger outlined the rationale for the 1972 agreements with the shah in these words:

> Under the Shah's leadership, the land bridge between Asia and Europe, so often the hinge of world history, was pro-American and pro-West beyond any challenge. Alone among the countries of the region--Israel aside--Iran made friendship with the United States the starting point of its policy. That it was based on a cold-eyed assessment that a threat to Iran would most likely come from the Soviet Union, in combination with radical Arab states, is only another way of saying that the Shah's view of the realities of world politics paralleled our own.[8]

Nixon, indeed, said to the shah at the end of their meeting: "Protect me." Once the shah had agreed to do so, Nixon sent a memo to the Washington foreign affairs bureaucracy instructing it that future Iranian requests for arms "should not be second-guessed." What the shah wanted, he was to get. And he wanted a lot, especially after the oil crisis of 1973 multiplied his government's revenues. For his part, the shah was delighted to be free of the restraints on his appetite for arms previously imposed by more cautious American administrations and could thus look forward to transforming Iran into the dominant power in the region. During the next four years, he ordered more than $9 billion in weapons, making Iran America's best customer for arms exports.

American deference to the shah extended beyond weapons to intelligence. The CIA dismantled many of its own operations in Iran, and thus became more and more reliant on SAVAK, the shah's feared secret police, for information about internal events. When American officials, State or CIA, did hazard contacts with the shah's domestic opponents, they often bumped into SAVAK or the court ministry. Henry Precht, the Iran desk officer in the State Department in 1977-1978, recalled that once when "one of our political officers went to talk to a mullah [a Muslim religious leader], we got word back that the shah's court ministry learned of this and didn't think it was a good idea."[9] Pressure not to probe into domestic affairs also came from above and began very early in the Nixon administration. Thus, as national security assistant, Henry Kissinger allegedly cancelled the US government's 1969 review of Iran on the grounds that it was an unnecessary intrusion into internal Iranian politics.

In these circumstances, the quality of American intelligence--both covert and open--on Iran declined steadily. A 1978 postmortem by the House Intelligence Committee described State Department political reporting on the Iranian opposition as "rare and sometimes contemptuous" and noted that the CIA provided not a single report based on sources within the Muslim religious opposition between 1975 and late 1977.

The transformation of the US-Iranian relationship under Nixon and Ford was dramatic. In the summer of 1976 the inspector general of the American Foreign Service reported that "the government of Iran exerts the determining influence" in relations with the United States. The preponderance of funding for joint efforts was Iranian, and "he who pays the piper calls the tune."[10]

The Carter Administration

When Jimmy Carter succeeded Gerald Ford in the White House in 1977, he was faced with competing commitments. On the one hand, he had pledged himself to make human rights a foundation of American foreign policy, and the shah's many critics were persistent in their demands that Carter require improvements in human rights in Iran. The shah himself was reportedly apprehensive that Carter might have "Kennedy-type pretensions"--that is, might press him for reform as Kennedy had in the early 1960s--and he made little secret of his hope that Gerald Ford would be elected instead of Carter.[11]

On the other hand, Carter was aware of American dependence on Persian Gulf oil and of the need for stability in the Middle East as a whole if he was to have a chance of pursuing a comprehensive settlement of the Arab-Israeli conflict.

Carter initially seemed inclined to follow through on his commitment to use pressure on foreign governments, friendly as well as unfriendly, to stop torture, political imprisonment, and other abuses of human rights. But in the Iranian case, pressure took the form of quiet suggestions. On the issue of arms supplies, Carter upset both the shah and Congress by his handling of an Iranian request for radar equipment. An Iranian request for ground-based radar stations was pending at the beginning of 1977, but the Carter administration decided instead to offer the sophisticated airborne warning and control system (AWACS) aircraft then coming into the US Air Force. The offer, however, was meant to betoken restraint in arms sales as well as support for the shah--Iran's request for ten planes was pared to seven.

However, in July 1977 the House Foreign Affairs Committee rejected the sale as contrary to the president's own promises. Moreover, the AWACS aircraft not only provided warning; they also could manage an air battle--for instance, against Israel. The rejection stung the shah's pride and his confidence in his ally, and he considered withdrawing the request altogether. The White House made a major effort to allay congressional concerns over the AWACS capability and security in the hands of Iran, and in October 1977 Congress approved the sale of the seven planes. Congress protested but did not stop other sales of sophisticated fighter planes.

Overall, Carter made no fundamental change in the special relationship created by his predecessor. Indeed, he gave the shah solid endorsements during the difficult November 1977 visit and again when the two men met in Tehran on New Year's Day 1978. Iran, Carter said on this occasion, was "an island of stability in a turbulent corner of the world"--a tribute that neither his critics nor the shah's enemies ever allowed him to forget.

THE REGIME UNDER ATTACK

(I)

Even as the president and the shah were cementing the US-Iranian alliance, the stability of the shah's rule was being challenged. To some extent, the challenge was encouraged by Carter's own emphasis on human rights. The shah's opponents--ever ready to believe in the omnipotence of the United States--took his declarations on the subject as evidence that international support for the shah was waning.[12]

But the sources of opposition antedated Carter's arrival in power--they lay in the "White Revolution" and the radical disturbances in Iranian society that had preceded it. The pace of modernization had sparked opposition from conservative clerics as early as 1963, when riots in the Shi'ite Muslim religious center of Qom were rigorously suppressed and the shah's severest critic, an ayatollah named Ruhollah Khomeini, was first exiled and then expelled from the country. With the leader of the conservative opposition out of circulation, the clerics remained quiescent for over a decade, and objections to the shah's rule and policies were muted by a repressive police force and by the benefits that accompanied the nation's newfound prosperity.[13]

As the economic boom slowed in the mid-1970s, cracks began to appear in the structure of the shah's regime. Economic and social change had not been accompanied by the development of political structures capable of articulating the concerns felt by significant elements of the population over the pace and direction of reform, mounting corruption, and the authoritarian nature of the shah's rule. Opposition came both from members of the Westernized elite, who supported the shah's efforts to propel Iran into the twentieth century but sought a more open and democratic political system, and from religious conservatives, whose principal target was the reform effort that secular opponents of the regime wished to preserve.[14]

To many foreign observers, the differences within the opposition were as deep as those between the government and its critics. As one diplomat noted: "It was impossible [in 1975] to see how [the] disparate elements of opposition could combine to unseat a powerful and resolute monarch, buttressed by strong and united armed services. There was not, as I saw it, a revolutionary situation in the country."[15] Unlike Somoza in Nicaragua or Marcos in the Philippines, the shah's regime seemed to be firmly institutionalized. It was more formidable than simply a dictator, or a family, with attached cronies: "To all intents and purposes, the Shah was at the centre of a series of circles, between which there was little contact except through him--the Court, the Imperial Family, the central government, the system of provincial government, the armed forces, SAVAK and the police. All these institutions functioned independently of each other and each reported directly to the Shah."[16] Yet such centralization had obvious costs, not the least being that it provided the opposition with a clear focus and a target on which all could agree. Despite their deep differences, the diverse groups within the opposition found one thing on which they could all agree: The real problem was the shah. Some moderates among both the secular and clerical opposition would have been happy to settle for a constitutional monarchy, though Reza Pahlevi had become personally unacceptable because of the excesses of SAVAK. Others wanted no part of Pahlevi rule, though these "others" covered every political shading from the Tudeh's advocacy of a Communist regime to the Islamic model presented by fundamentalist clerics.[17]

However they assessed the shah's government or its chances of survival, most Americans (not to mention the shah's own secret police) dismissed the clerics as a serious threat. For the Americans, as for many moderate Iranians, religious fundamentalism was simply not seen as a serious issue in Iran. The shah, after all, had been intent for nearly two decades on a modernization program that included such Western ideas as secular rule and the emancipation of women, leaving little political role for religion. The power of the clerics had seemingly been broken by the shah in 1963, when Khomeini was sent into exile. Iranian Prime Minister Jamshid Amouzegar reflected this mindset (which possessed the secular opposition as well) when he commented in 1977 that "the reactionary mullahs are finished; Iran has moved beyond them." Or, as one American official later remarked, "Who ever took religion seriously?"[18]

The danger of such a view should have been apparent from the speed with which the fundamentalists gathered mass support and the skill with which they directed it against the shah. On January 7, 1978, for example, the government-sponsored paper, *Ettelaat*, ridiculed the Ayatollah Khomeini. This attack coincided with the end of the holy month of Moharram when religious passion among the Shi'ites was at a particularly high pitch. Two days later, a large protest march took place in the city of Qom, the Shi'ite center from which Khomeini had been sent into exile fourteen years earlier. Twenty demonstrators were killed as the police fired on the crowd. When, as Islamic custom required, the Shi'ites commemorated the casualties of Qom at forty-day intervals throughout the remainder of 1978, ever larger demonstrations occurred--a cycle later dubbed by an official of the Khomeini government who had taken part in them, "doing the 40-40." The government met the demonstrations with increased repression; opposition leaders' houses were bombed and the leaders were beaten up by vigilante groups widely believed to be connected with SAVAK.

Despite the regularity and ever-increasing scale of the fundamentalist demonstrations, the shah displayed no public doubts that he would prevail over the opposition. In a June 1978 interview headlined, "Nobody Can Overthrow Me--I Have the Power," the shah ascribed the demonstrations to religious reaction to his own reform measures and to external subversion:

> In some cases, it is a matter of personal vengeance against me. There is the religious reaction of some of the Moslem priests against our programs of modernization. The Communists are also active, and we have the strange phenomenon here of the reactionary groups and the leftists working together. . . . Nobody can overthrow me. I have the support of 700,000 troops, all the workers and most of the people. Wherever I go, there are fantastic demonstrations of support. I have the power, and the opposition cannot be compared in strength with the government in any way.[19]

To the British Ambassador, the shah seemed quite confident in his ability to prevail, though he had begun to attack the very middle-class critics whom he had hoped to co-opt through modernization. In March 1978, he told Parsons that he "did not particularly fear the communists and other radical elements drawn from the student body. The National Front and the other old political parties were not a serious threat. His most implacable enemies, and the most powerful, were the mullahs with their hold on the minds of the masses. There could be no compromise with them. . . . They could neither be bought nor could they be negotiated into co-operation with a regime which they did not recognise."[20]

At this point, the shah was determined to continue with a liberalization he had decided upon partly to appease the Americans, and partly to create a political base for the transfer of power to his son. His approach, however, rested on the assumption that he could reverse such liberalization when he wished and, in reversing it, could suppress the political appetites it had stimulated. As the summer wore on, it became obvious that this assumption was flawed and that the approach overall entailed a loss of initiative on the part of the shah: liberalization, in Parsons' words, "amounted to a tactic without an overall strategy."[21]

The opposition itself might not be united on goals and strategy, but it grew simply by exploiting opportunities, some of them presented by the religious calendar. Thus when the holy month of Ramadan began on August 5, a new wave of demonstrations spread across Iran. Even disasters offered possibilities for agitation against the shah. On August 19, a fire swept through a movie theater in Abadan, killing 477 when exit doors turned out to be locked. The government and opposition charged each other with setting the fire, and the perpetrators were never caught. The incident served to incite more violence.

At the end of August, the shah turned to a new government, a "reform" cabinet headed by Prime Minister Ja'far Sharif-Emami, who had held the same job in the early 1960s. During his earlier tenure, he had promised political participation to the opposition, favored the Islamic calendar, and had moved against corrupt "Western" institutions such as casinos. Still, his many critics saw him as ineffectual, corrupt, and tied to the monarchy. His second tenure was no more successful than his first. After Sharif-Emami had been in office for two months, Iran's universities still remained closed and strikes in the oil industry had not been settled.

Opposition groups marked the end of Ramadan with large demonstrations in Tehran on September 4 and 5. The success of those demonstrations prompted calls for a general strike, to which the government responded by declaring martial law, announced on the evening of September 7. The next morning, twenty thousand people congregated in Tehran's Jaleh Square for a rally against the shah. When the crowd ignored orders to disperse, government troops opened fire. The shooting went on and on, and broke out around Tehran throughout the day. Casualty estimates varied wildly, from over one hundred killed to one thousand.

Foreign Views of the Crisis

By the summer of 1978, foreign observers of Iran were noting the signs of breakdown in Iran's internal stability, but none was yet prepared to predict flatly that the shah would fall. A junior French diplomat expressed the view that the shah would not survive, and a senior Israeli representative in Iran, Uri Lubrani, cabled Tel Aviv in June 1978 that the shah might not last as long as two or three years. Lubrani later indicated that he had discussed his assessment with the American ambassador to Iran, William Sullivan, but Sullivan's June cable to Washington, the result of an embassy review, included neither Lubrani's conclusions nor those of the French officer. Soon thereafter Sullivan returned to Washington for home leave, still expressing confidence in the shah.

In Washington, nobody at a senior level was prepared to contemplate the possibility of the shah's government collapsing or the implications of such a collapse. Indeed, at the time of the Jaleh Square massacre, nobody at a senior level was even prepared to discuss Iran. As in the Nicaraguan case, the president and his foreign policy advisers were engrossed in the Camp David summit involving Carter, President Sadat of Egypt, and Prime Minister Begin of Israel. After news of the massacre arrived, Henry Precht, the Iran desk officer at the State Department, could not get the attention of Harold Saunders, the assistant secretary of state for Near Eastern and South Asian affairs.

This problem of indifference abroad continued throughout the fall and extended to many other governments. John D. Stempel, a political officer at the US embassy in Tehran, later remarked that this refusal to recognize the possibility of the shah's falling continued until the establishment of a military government in early November:

> Prior to November 5 . . . with the exception of the American, French, Israeli, British, and possibly the Soviet embassies, no country had an in-depth understanding of how badly the trend of events was going against the Shah. Individuals in each of these missions had detected patterns that spelled trouble, but in no case had the decision making process of the country involved assimilated that information and converted it into policy actions. Prescient Western analysts found their home office bureaucracies still convinced that either the Shah or the military or both would prevent a revolution from occurring.[22]

Even when policymakers could be induced to consider the Iranian problem, they lacked detailed information about what was in any case a turbulent and fluid situation. Their natural reluctance to "make the call" against the shah was reinforced by the pattern of almost reflexive American support for him. The extent of US reliance on the shah not only had eliminated incentives to maintain independent sources of information, it also had made his downfall too unpleasant to contemplate. Henry Precht's description of the attitude of Zbigniew Brzezinski, the president's national security adviser, is representative: "Brzezinski simply wanted to see the Shah's regime remain, wanted to see us support him, and wasn't going to hear anything that contradicted that position. 'Tell me how to make it work,' his position seemed to be."[23]

Moreover, Washington's institutional memory was reassuring where the shah himself was concerned. Old Iran-hands remembered the troubles of the 1960s. Then, the shah had been able to "jump ahead of the opposition" with his White Revolution, as Saunders had put it, so why not now? Those events and the early 1970s had led Washington to the belief that the shah was tough-minded and decisive. Ambassador Sullivan found a very different person:

> From the briefings I had received in Washington and the "psychological profiles" I had read concerning the monarch, I expected a rather arrogant man, masking his insecurity in pompous pronouncements. The man I met was anything but that. He spoke in a quiet tone, maintained a modest demeanor, and was quite candid, almost tentative in the manner in which he presented his conclusions, and rather gentle in his courtesies. . . . I came to the conclusion that the external image of the haughty autocrat that had been cultivated by his court and promulgated by his critics was not an accurate one. He was not truly cast to be a leader of men or the nation in time of crisis.[24]

In 1978, the shah's indecision was almost certainly increased by one particular matter that he kept secret, even from his closest relatives--the fact that he was suffering from cancer.

The increasing turmoil in Iran did not set off alarm bells in the American intelligence community. The effort to produce a National Intelligence Estimate (NIE) on Iran, the government's premier agreed assessment, ran into the sand over the summer. The CIA's only forecasting on a "post-shah Iran" dealt exclusively with the mechanics of a transition *within* the Pahlavi dynasty.

On September 10, Carter--who throughout the period was reluctant to call the shah--telephoned the Iranian ruler to express his support for him. Carter also encouraged the shah not to let his liberalization program flag. The shah agreed and asked the president to reiterate his public support. Soon afterwards, the White House released a statement describing the call and reaffirming the close ties between Iran and the United States; the statement was read over the air on Tehran Radio. Under the circumstances, however, the statement, intended to strengthen the shah's hand, probably served more to identify the United States with the Jaleh Square massacre.

Moreover, it did not reassure the shah, who was perpetually concerned about foreign powers (particularly the United States and Britain) undermining him. Late in September, the British ambassador found him "worried that the Americans might be plotting with the opposition."[25] Parsons told him this not so, adding that the real sources of his troubles were internal: "I even doubted [Parsons remarked] whether the Soviet Union was actively supporting the movement to overthrow the regime. . . . My assessment was that they would prefer to have an orderly Iran under the Shah on their long southern frontier than an unpredictable Iran under whatever regime might replace him."[26]

Within Iran, troubles continued to multiply. Pilgrims returning to Iran from the holy city of Najaf, Ayatollah Khomeini's place of exile in Iraq, brought back cassettes of his sermons attacking the shah. Those cassettes were played in mosques all over Iran almost immediately. The shah responded by putting pressure on Iraq to curtail Khomeini's activities. Iraq agreed, and on October 6 Khomeini left Iraq for Paris.[27]

The Iranian government expected that distance would mute the force of Khomeini's anti-shah efforts, but it, and almost everyone else, failed to anticipate how modern technology had changed the politics of revolution. Simply by using the direct-dial telephone, Khomeini continued to direct his lieutenants in Iran. Moreover, the ayatollah, then well into his seventies and a medievalist with no life experience outside Shi'ia Islam, became the darling of Western journalists. Street demonstrations increased rather than abated after Khomeini moved to Paris, as the forty-day mourning date for the Jaleh Square dead approached.

By mid-October Precht and his colleagues at the working level of the State Department were worried enough to put their concerns on paper. Their paper recommended continuing support for the shah but recognized the worsening violence in Iran and the ineffectiveness of the shah's response. It found no evidence that the existing track of US support for the shah had influenced events. The paper concluded that the shah had to establish an effective government "within a few weeks" but ruled out a military government as likely only to incite the shah's opponents. Without suggesting what, if any, specific advice the United States should give the shah, the State Department paper "left open for possible future consideration the possibility of initiating contacts with Khomeini and the opposition forces as well as the possibility of sending a special envoy to the Shah as a dramatic expression of US support."[28]

Asked to comment on the working-level paper, Sullivan argued against any dramatic change in policy. Quiet reassurance was more important than expressions of high-level support for the shah. In comments dated October 27, he outlined his own efforts to persuade political moderates to enter the Iranian system. His conclusion mirrored the prevailing mind-set in Washington. Firmly rejecting any overture to Khomeini, Sullivan declared: "Our destiny is to work with the Shah."[29]

In view of Sullivan's objections, the working-level document was quietly interred in the State Department: President Carter saw neither the working paper nor Sullivan's response to it. Indeed, as October drew to a close, "there had still not been a single high-level policy meeting in Washington on this subject."[30]

Within days, the shah himself seemed to be having doubts about whether he could manage the turmoil.[31] His immediate strategy involved trying to divide the opposition by co-opting the liberal opposition, represented by the National Front (a broad secular reform movement of the moderate left that had backed Mossadeq in 1953). The shah toyed with appointing one of the aged leaders of the National Front as prime minister in place of the unpopular Sharif-Emami. But the main NF leaders had gone to France to try to persuade Khomeini to accept preservation of the monarchy in return for substantial constitutional reform. Khomeini absolutely refused to consider any continuation of the monarchy.

In a November 1 meeting with Sullivan and the British ambassador, Sir Anthony Parsons, the shah said he would rather leave Iran than submit to a referendum on the monarchy--one of the demands of the National Front. The next day, Sullivan reported on the meeting to Washington and added a comment through restricted channels, noting the shah's remark hinting at abdication. He believed the shah would seek American advice about whether to abdicate or impose a military government. Parsons, for his part, believed that events had now moved beyond orthodox political maneuvering and somewhat beyond the shah's own control. Since mid-October, it had been clear to him that "the focus of political activity had moved outside the recognised institutions of Shah, government and parliament."[32] The shah's own comment on his situation was poignant enough: "We are melting away daily like snow in water."[33]

EXERCISES

Set up one or more working groups (identically composed) with represen-
tatives from the State Department (including the Iran desk officer and the assis-
tant secretary for Near East and South Asian affairs), the National Security
Council, the CIA, and the Department of Defense to consider the following
agenda and draft a short (3-4 page) position paper:

1. On the evidence available up to this point, *what are the short-term and*
   medium-term prospects for the shah's survival as head of state of Iran?
   How adequate is our knowledge of current developments in Iran? What
   kinds of issue are particularly difficult to assess? What kinds of important
   information are either lacking or suspect as available?
2. *What courses of action are open to the shah? What are the costs and bene-*
   fits and the specific feasibility of each? What does current evidence suggest
   about the likelihood of his taking particular courses? Absent any action by
   the shah, what is likely to happen?
3. *How are American interests likely to be affected by particular strategies,*
   whether adopted by the shah, by his allies, or by his opponents? Regardless
   of strategies, how will particular outcomes affect US interests?
4. *What should the United States be trying to achieve in the current situation?*
   What kinds of intervention by US representatives might be effective? What
   instructions should be given to the US ambassador?

THE REGIME UNDER ATTACK

(II)

Sullivan's comment finally stirred senior Washington foreign policy officials to consider Iran. On November 2, the National Security Council's
Special Coordination Committee (SCC) met at the White House to respond
to Sullivan's request for instructions. Brzezinski chaired the meeting, the
other main participants in which were Deputy Secretary of State Warren
Christopher; Secretary of Defense Harold Brown; General David Jones, the
chairman of the joint chiefs of staff; and Admiral Stansfield Turner, the director of central intelligence. Brzezinski reported on conversations with the
president and with the shah's ambassador in Washington (and former son-in-

law), Ardeshir Zahedi, and he presented a draft message for Sullivan to take to the shah.

The message reflected Brzezinski's view that the chaos in Iran called for strong action, perhaps including military rule. It expressed unconditional American support for the shah, noted the need for "decisive action" to restore order, and encouraged the resumption of liberalization once order had been restored. After some discussion and modification, the SCC approved the message. Brzezinski telephoned the shah the next day to assure him of Washington's firm support, and Vance stressed the same point publicly at a news conference.

Any disagreement occurring at this point between Brzezinski and the State Department, including Vance, initially was less one about ends than means, for both Brzezinski and Vance wanted the shah to remain on his throne. As the situation in Iran deteriorated, however, the agreement on ends became much less important than the disagreement over means.

Brzezinski advocated a tough response, a military government if need be, throughout the Iranian crisis, employing both the power of his argument and a variety of bureaucratic stratagems to try to persuade his government. He had been influenced, he later wrote, by the historian of revolutions, Crane Brinton: "I felt strongly that successful revolutions were historical rarities, that they were inevitable only after they happened, and that an established leadership, by demonstrating both will and reason, could disarm the opposition through a timely combination of repression and concession."[34]

For Brzezinski, conciliation--which he characterized as a "quaint notion favored by American lawyers of liberal bent"--might have worked in Iran two years before but not in 1978 when the crisis was acute.

Brzezinski's views were reinforced through his contacts with Zahedi, which became more and more frequent during 1978. Like Brzezinski, Zahedi thought Iran's turmoil required a military clamp-down. Zahedi's ties to the shah dated back to 1953 when his father had played a major role in restoring the shah to his throne. He himself was a figure to be reckoned with in Iranian politics. Many in the shah's inner circle believed that Zahedi coveted the prime ministership, and the shah himself was disparaging about Zahedi's activities and his political sense.[35] Through Zahedi--whom Brzezinski described as "a useful source of information"--Brzezinski was able to keep his views in front of the shah during the late months of 1978. Zahedi also used the contact to his advantage, leaving many in Iran uncertain whether he spoke for himself or reflected White House views.

Indeed, when Zahedi returned to Tehran, he immediately called Ambassador Sullivan to his home. In Sullivan's words: "He took me into his study and in his most conspiratorial tone told me that 'Brzezinski has taken over Iran policy.' He described how he had been summoned to the White House by Brzezinski and been told that the Shah needed to be stiffened in his resolve."[36] Zahedi told Sullivan that when he had resisted Brzezinski's urging to return to Iran, he had been taken to President Carter "who told him that he, President Carter, would be the Iranian ambassador in Washington and that Zahedi should feel it was his primary duty to return to Tehran and stiffen the shah's spine."[37]

On November 4, the shah summoned both Sullivan and Parsons to the palace. According to Parsons, "The Shah opened by telling us that he had received a telephone call from Zbigniew Brzezinski [who] had told him that the US government would support him either for the formation of a coalition government or a military government. . . . Sullivan made clear that Brzezinski's phone call did not mean that the United States favoured the military option, rather that they would go along with it if the Shah decided that he had absolutely no other choice."[38] In the discussion that followed, the shah explained that he was still trying to arrange a coalition involving the National Front and that he was under pressure from his generals to arrest the leaders of the opposition. He went on to say that "it was all very well for Brzezinski to talk, but he still believed that unleashing the generals would solve nothing."[39] Parsons agreed, predicting that a military crackdown ("whatever that meant") would simply provoke a national strike. Belatedly, as official Washington began to realize that the scale of dissent in Iran was running well beyond its expectations, the quality of intelligence became an issue. On November 6, Sick wrote Brzezinski that "the most fundamental problem at the moment is the astonishing lack of hard information we are getting about developments in Iran."[40] Carter had raised the issue of intelligence with Vance just before Sick's note and raised it again with CIA Director Turner at a Policy Review Committee meeting. Turner acknowledged the problem but said there was little in the short term he could do about it because of the reduction of American intelligence capabilities in Iran during the 1970s.[41]

While Washington debated intelligence, tensions rose in Iran. By early November, strikes by refinery and oil-field workers and by civil servants were costing the country $60 million per day. Emami's reconciliation efforts came to nothing, and he resigned on November 5, after anti-shah demonstrators rampaged through Tehran setting fire to buildings. The shah ordered the military to restore order and placed the country under military rule. An eleven-member cabinet headed by armed forces chief General Gholam Riza Azhari quickly arrested several prominent SAVAK officials and business leaders, and ordered striking oil workers to return to their jobs. Most did return, but the calm was brief. Late in November, workers in major cities heeded a call by Shi'ia leaders for a one-day strike. From Paris, Khomeini then called for an indefinite strike.

The shah's approach to the political crisis was, in the eyes of many observers, curiously passive and at times confusing. While formally supporting Azhari's efforts to restore law and order, the shah engaged in a series of negotiations through intermediaries (including his own chauffeur) with members of the opposition (and almost exclusively the oldest among them) in an effort to coopt his rivals. These efforts went on without any consultation with his own government.

At the same time, Zahedi, with the backing of Brzezinski, was trying to organize a movement of loyalists drawn from the more conservative senior officers of the armed forces, Tehran merchants, and clergy hostile to Khomeini. The shah himself told Sullivan that Zahedi's efforts were misguided and asked him "to inform Washington that Zahedi did not understand the domestic situation in Iran."[42]

In his negotiations, the shah declared himself ready to hold truly free elections, to empower parliament to name the prime minister, and to allow the government to control the budget. But he refused (at least until mid-December) to concede command of the armed forces or to let parliament control the military budget.[43]

The one constant in the shah's responses was his reluctance to use force or, indeed, to assert himself in the way that the Iranian establishment expected. His reluctance seems to have been partly an expression of a genuine concern about breaking the tie with "his people," partly a reflection of his fear that repression would strengthen the extremists among the religious leaders and the left. But it also was an effect of his physical state and the psychological condition in which his medication left him. Visitors frequently found him withdrawn and dejected, though on other occasions he seemed to have completely recovered and to be in full control.

The Ambassador's Dilemma

Observing the lethargic posture of the shah, the ineffectuality of his political maneuvers, and the increasing dominance of Khomeini over the opposition, Ambassador Sullivan abandoned his previously optimistic view of the regime's future. Though as recently as October 27 he had argued that destiny had cast the United States in the role of cooperating with the shah, by November 9 he had shifted view. In a long cable to Washington entitled

"Thinking the Unthinkable," he argued that the Azhari government represented the last chance for the shah. He had (now and increasingly later) little confidence in the political grasp of the shah or the value of his maneuvers: "All the steps the Shah was willing to take politically [Sullivan commented] were always too little and too late. In retrospect it is improbable that any action he might have taken would have defused the revolution. In fact, by the time he was brought to contemplate these measures, the revolution had accumulated such momentum that it is unlikely it could have been averted."[44]

Given this view of the regime, Sullivan was naturally concerned about what would happen if the Azhari government failed. Earlier than his superiors, he suggested that the United States should start to anticipate the collapse of the shah and begin "to examine some options which we have never before considered relevant."[45]

Sullivan's analysis was distinguished by an explicit emphasis on protecting "our national interests in Iran" and by a concern to prevent the Soviet Union from taking advantage of instability in Iran. As he put it in his memoirs: "My assumption was a contingency in which the Shah would lose power, and my purpose, in that contingency, was to try to preserve a working relationship for the United States that would preempt Soviet opportunities flowing from a successful revolution."[46] Sullivan's analysis assumed that the central question was increasingly that of the relationship between the military and the religious opposition. Like the shah (but unlike Brzezinski), he felt that the use of the military to repress the religious opposition would not end the revolution. The alternative was some kind of accommodation between the military and the armed forces. Such an accommodation, Sullivan thought, might occur without too much conflict and might even have consequences that would be "essentially satisfactory" for American interests.[47]

The condition that would force such an accommodation would be the departure of the shah and some senior officers. With a "new, younger military leadership" in charge, Sullivan predicted, "Ayatollah Khomeini would have to choose a government headed by moderate figures like Bazargan and Minatchi [of the Liberation Front, a political ally of the ayatollahs' and eschew the 'Nasser-Qadhafi' types which I assumed he would prefer."[48] The religious leaders would settle for such a regime since they would have got rid of the shah, avoided a bloody confrontation with the military, and would, indeed, have secured control of the state. As for US interests, Sullivan noted: "From our point of view, it would be satisfactory because it would avoid chaos, ensure the continued integrity of the country, preclude a radical leadership, and effectively block Soviet domination of the Persian Gulf. In these circumstances, the major losses, as I saw them, would be a reduction in the intimacy of our military and security relations, a shift on Iran's part from a pro-Israeli to an anti-Zionist position, and a certain aloofness in our overall dealings."[49] Such costs might be acceptable if the alternative was the disintegration of the Iranian armed forces and severe civil conflict, both of which would virtually invite Soviet interference.

Sullivan's cable did not, however, directly recommend that the US government begin to withdraw its support for the shah, much less that it advise him to abdicate. (Indeed, while advocating that Washington start "thinking about the unthinkable," it reportedly concluded that to continue trusting the shah to face down Khomeini was "obviously the only safe course to pursue at this juncture."[50])

Although (in Sullivan's view) his cable alerted President Carter for the first time to the possibility that the shah might lose his throne, it did not lead to better or more frequent communication between Washington and the Tehran embassy. Sullivan subsequently complained that he was a victim of indifference on the part of his superiors. He had, he said, "received no specific political guidance about the attitude of the government of the United States" toward the changing circumstances of the shah's regime and the political maneuvers in which he was engaged.[51] Although Washington repeatedly made statements in support of the shah and sent private emissaries to Tehran, Sullivan himself was unable to get a clear response to his cable of November 9.[52] When the ambassador expressed his pessimism about the future of the regime to the press, he was reminded by Washington "that the United States government's policy was to support the Shah and that [he] should avoid undermining that policy in [his] relations with the press."[53]

Brzezinski and his assistant Gary Sick later blamed Sullivan for failing to alert them early enough to the seriousness of the shah's situation and for changing his assessment abruptly.[54] Brzezinski emphasized that Sullivan had not in fact sought instructions (he was regarded in Washington as an ambassador who guarded his autonomy jealously). Moreover, his assessment of the situation up to this point had actually been more reassuring than that which Brzezinski was getting from Sick. Sullivan had, indeed, previously been almost "obsequious" toward the shah and had advised against any approach to Khomeini.[55] After the appointment of Azhari, Sullivan (in Brzezinski's view) continually diluted Washington's exhortations to the shah to act "decisively" against the opposition and engaged in negotiations with the opposition that were both futile and subversive of the shah's credibility.

Sick, somewhat more gently, suggests that Sullivan failed to warn Washington of the possible collapse of the shah and failed to clearly declare "the moment of truth" when it arrived:

On three different occasions, Sullivan rejected suggestions from the Department of State that he take a more active stance of advising the Shah and building contacts with the moderate opposition. Instead, he attempted to walk a perilous line between declaratory support for the Shah in his reporting cables while conducting private negotiations with the opposition for plans that were to be implemented only after the Shah decided to leave. In the end, this policy produced the worst of both worlds. His support for the Shah was perceived in Washington and Tehran as equivocal, thereby undercutting his credibility in both camps.[56]

In Sick's view, Sullivan's "Thinking the Unthinkable" cable was fatally inconclusive: It "permitted him to ruminate about policy without committing himself to any controversial positions . . . the message was cleverly written, but it may have been too clever by half."[57]

But Brzezinski and Sick were by now aware that Sullivan had sympathizers in Washington, and that they were heavily concentrated in the State Department. Henry Precht (the desk officer for Iran) and several others at State had reached a view about the shah essentially similar to Sullivan's, their disenchantment with his rule having been sharpened by the human rights concerns of the new administration. In these circumstances, their willingness to contemplate what Precht called "a soft landing, using the Shah to effect some kind of transition" gained them the reputation of being "anti-Shah."[58]

However, this group differed from Sullivan and others in the Tehran embassy in that its members still thought that the National Front politicians enjoyed enough support to be able to stand up to the revolutionaries. Sullivan notes: "We in the embassy did not agree. We did not think they had any constituency. We thought they would be rolled over by the revolution."[59]

In any case, Precht and his colleagues had, as Sick put it, "no one to carry their arguments from the State Department to the White House. They became frustrated and angry and were reduced to a form of guerrilla warfare to try to get the word out"--a state of affairs that continued even after late November when the SCC created, as had been its custom for other "hot" issues, a "mini-SCC," chaired by Brzezinski's deputy, David Aaron, to serve as the focal point for policymaking at the senior staff level.[60] But Precht and his colleagues were still in the dark regarding the advice given to the White House.

The Ball Report

In December, the administration turned to the first of a series of high-level "outsiders" for help--George Ball, an investment banker, Kennedy's undersecretary of state, and pillar of the liberal foreign policy establishment since Roosevelt's time. Ball--who had "reluctantly concluded that the shah was on the way to a great fall and that, like Humpty-Dumpty, his regime could not be put together again,"[61] and who had expressed that view to private New York gatherings in September and October--was suggested to Carter by Michael Blumenthal, the secretary of the treasury. Sick, assigned by Brzezinski to serve as Ball's aide, first met Ball on December 1. Ball's incisive questions over four hours convinced Sick that "Ball would produce some fresh insights about the situation but that they would not be what Brzezinski wanted to hear."[62]

December 2 marked the beginning of the holy month of Moharram, watched with apprehension in both Tehran and Washington. Demonstrations involved hundreds of thousands, and several times ran out of control; in Tehran and Isfahan demonstrators were killed. Strikes by oil workers reduced production to record low levels and fed the flight of capital from Iranian banks.

In these circumstances, casual remarks by the president at a breakfast meeting with reporters caused a sensation in the world press and plunged the shah into deep depression. When asked if the shah could ride out the crisis, Carter replied: "I don't know. I hope so. This is something that is in the hands of the people of Iran. . . . We personally prefer that the Shah maintain a major role in the government, but that is a decision for the Iranian people to make."[63] For Carter the remark may have been little more than a statement of American principles. But for Iranians, both in government and in opposition, who were accustomed to reading Washington's entrails for signals, it was taken as an indication that the United States intended to dump the shah. A stream of clarifications and restatements issued in the following days in Washington could not change the impression thus created.

Ball confined his review to Washington, having "learned from our Vietnam experience how dangerous it can be when travel is substituted for thought."[64] "My sudden appearance in Tehran [he noted] would merely provide new documentation for those attacking the shah as subservient to America."[65] While Ball worked in Washington, Sullivan saw more and more of the shah as the shah debated how to restore order. On December 12, he told Sullivan that, in view of Khomeini's popularity in Iran, he saw three options: continuing to try to form a national coalition; surrendering to the opposition, leaving a regency council in charge; and forming a military junta to put down the opposition with force.

The shah was pessimistic about all three options. Sullivan held to the lines of his cable a month earlier, urging the shah to continue negotiations with the moderate opposition, especially the National Front. Sullivan resisted State Department suggestions that he play a more visible political role in Tehran; he still believed maneuvering behind the scenes would be more effective, and he feared that activism would only make the United States more of a target.

Ball submitted his report to the president the same day as Sullivan met with the shah in Tehran. The report concluded that the shah's regime was "on the verge of collapse. We must make clear," Ball continued, "that, in our view, his only chance to save his dynasty (if indeed that is still possible) and retain our support is for him to transfer his power to a government responsive to the people."[66] In view of "growing discontent particularly among junior officers," any attempt to use the army to restore order would fail; the army would disintegrate. The problem was to provide a mechanism for the shah to transfer power without discrediting the recipient as the shah's own creature. To that end, Ball suggested a "Council of Notables," perhaps fifty Iranians carefully chosen to represent all opposition groups except the extreme left. The council would not be a government, but it would choose one.

Brzezinski (as Sick had predicted) did not like what he heard from Ball. Indeed, he now regretted having agreed to Ball's involvement. It had merely, he later wrote, "sharpened our disagreements while delaying basic choices by wasting some two weeks, and his subsequent willingness to discuss what transpired within the White House and the State Department with members of the press spiced the perception of an Administration profoundly split on the Iranian issue."[67] Brzezinski felt that he had violated a basic rule of bureaucratic tactics: "One should never obtain the services of an 'impartial' outside consultant regarding an issue that one feels strongly about without first making certain in advance that one knows the likely contents of his advice."[68]

The SCC met to discuss the Ball report on the 13th, and the next day Ball met with Carter. Though the president agreed with much of Ball's diagnosis, he said he could not accept the council proposal: "I cannot tell another head of state what to do."[69]

In the meantime, another experienced official had weighed into the debate--Energy Secretary James Schlesinger, who had served as secretary of defense and director of the CIA in the previous administration and who had known the shah for some time. He shared Brzezinski's view that the collapse of the shah would be a strategic disaster for the United States. He lobbied the president's closest advisors--Hamilton Jordan, Jody Powell, and Charles Kirbo--to send a high-level emissary to Tehran to buck up the shah and underscore US support.

At Ball's meeting with the president, Carter mentioned this idea, suggesting Brzezinski as a possible emissary. Ball expressed his strong opposition, citing the reasons that had led him not to go to Iran. An emissary, he argued, would immobilize the shah entirely by making all his subsequent actions appear to be prompted by instructions from the United States.[70] Carter heeded Ball's advice, at least for the time being.

Ball was distressed by the state of policymaking as he had observed it, and he confided his worries to Vance, an old friend. He found "a shockingly unhealthy situation in the National Security Council, with Brzezinski doing everything possible to exclude the State Department from participation in, or even knowledge of, our developing relations with Iran, communicating directly with Zahedi to the exclusion of our embassy, and using so-called back channel [CIA channel] telegrams of which the State Department was unaware."[71] Vance replied angrily that Brzezinski had promised to stop using the back channel and said he would again try to put a stop to it.

Ball's report did convince the president that the Iranian crisis was urgent. On December 16, Sullivan was sent a message conveying the president's concern and listing a set of questions about conditions in Iran to be raised with the shah. When he met with Sullivan two days later, the shah said he was hoping to install a government of national unity--headed by Gholam Hussein Sadiqi, with whom he had just met--within two weeks. To Sick, reading the account of the meeting in Washington, the plan reflected the shah's loss of touch with what was going on in his country. A nationwide strike was underway, and the military was visibly coming apart, yet the shah was bargaining as he had for months--making marginal concessions but remaining unwilling to share real power.

NEGOTIATING THE SUCCESSION?

In the week before Christmas, both Precht and Sick independently reached the conclusion that the shah's collapse was imminent. At the time neither knew of the other's conclusions: Such was the state of cooperation between State and the NSC. On the 19th, Precht sent a long memorandum to Sullivan and Harold Saunders. The chances of the shah surviving, he wrote, were minimal, and so the United States should take steps to protect its interests in the transition to an Iran without the shah. His cover letter was candid, reflecting his own frustration: "I have probably confided more than I should to a piece of paper, but I doubt I have much of a future anyway."[72]

Two days later Sick pulled his boss, Brzezinski, out of a White House Christmas party. The Embassy had just cabled that General Azhari had been relieved of his military command after suffering a heart attack.[73] That, Sick believed, marked a critical turning point. He returned to his office to put his thoughts on paper. Unless an effective government were established within two weeks, Sick wrote, "the Shah and his dynasty are going to be swept away."[74] The talks with Hussein Sadiqi were a waste of time, Sick felt, and so the United States needed to press the shah to make a dramatic move quickly. A military regime would not work, he reckoned, because the military was too divided and because there was no political framework for military action.

Sullivan reached a similar conclusion, making his own inferences concerning future action. Concluding his report to Washington on his meeting with Azhari, he told his superiors that "the military government had failed in its mission to restore law and order. The downfall of the Shah was inevitable. Therefore, I intended to take the action I had prescribed in my November 9 cable and would begin talks with the opposition and the armed forces, designed to help them reach an accommodation that would prevent the disintegration of the military forces. I received no instructions as a result of this cable that would stop me from my proposed course of action."[75]

But neither Sick's nor Sullivan's warnings produced a change in policy. Precht suggested a council of notables along the lines of Ball's earlier proposal (of which he had not heard). In any event, his proposal met the same fate as Ball's. At the White House, Brzezinski did not yet share Sick's view that Iran was at the point of crisis. On the 21st Sullivan was instructed to continue supporting the shah's negotiations.

Events soon confirmed the dire warnings. The wave of strikes shut the oil industry down entirely by December 27. With gasoline and with heating oil reserves of only one week, a crisis was at hand, and the government announced rationing plans to prevent homes from freezing at night. Street demonstrations reached a crescendo the same day, as cars burned, merchants evacuated their stores, and tear gas filled the air. Iran received three-line headlines on the front page of the *New York Times* on the 28th and 30th, but the latter account reported that "there was no air of crisis in the administration." The administration did order a carrier task force to leave the Philippines for possible deployment to the Persian Gulf.

On December 29, the shah named opposition leader Shahpour Bakhtiar to head a new civilian government. Bakhtiar seemed to Sullivan a curious choice. A cultivated Francophile and a leader of one faction of the moderate National Front, Bakhtiar had, in the Embassy's view, "no popular following and . . . his ability to act like an effective political leader was almost nil."[76] More remarkably, when Sullivan discussed the Bakhtiar appointment with the shah, it turned out that the Iranian leader more than shared this view.[77]

Bakhtiar, however, had a grander view of his own destiny. It quickly became clear that he had misunderstood (or intended to ignore) the role that the shah and many others expected him to play. Whereas in the shah's eyes "Bakhtiar was intended to be nothing more than a fig leaf that would permit [the shah] to leave the country in good constitutional form," Bakhtiar felt that his mission was to "steal the revolution away" from Khomeini.[78] With the shah gone, he thought he could become a popular leader in his own right: The Iranian masses, he believed, were not entirely behind the ayatollah and his companions.

On January 1, 1979, Bakhtiar announced an ambitious reform program aiming at a "socially democratic society." However, even to rule the country he needed the support of the armed forces. Therefore, American officials regarded his choice of a minister of war as the most important. He chose General Fereidoun Jam, who had lived in exile for years after a dispute with the shah over using the military to repress domestic dissent and who was esteemed by his colleagues in the Iranian military. Jam, however, refused the job after a meeting with the shah.

Jam's refusal was a severe blow for Bakhtiar, for it suggested that his government was (as many observers had expected) merely a front for the shah. In fact, the ensuing weeks confirmed that image. It turned out that Jam had declined after the shah had refused to relinquish full control over the military. Jam had concluded that the Bakhtiar government would not have enough real authority to govern.

By early January, Washington had become convinced that the shah would have to leave Iran if the new government was to have any hope. The United States pressed him to agree to Bakhtiar's suggestion that he leave when the new government was installed, but the shah demurred. On January 2, he told Sullivan that he would leave for a rest, but only after law and order had been restored, his words implying that he expected the Bakhtiar government to fail at that task. The shah then debated aloud his two remaining options--the "iron fist" or a regency council--but visibly could not make up his mind. Sullivan left the meeting convinced that the United States would have to apply strong pressure to force a decision by the shah.

The National Security Council met the next day in Washington. Participants, men who had earlier been reluctant to conclude that the shah was on the way out, now were reluctant to push him. Some feared that his departure would alarm neighboring states, while others felt it would plunge Iran into civil war. Charles Duncan, the acting secretary of defense, suggested sending General Robert Huyser, the deputy commander of US forces in Europe, to Iran. His mission was to try to keep the Iranian military together, urging them to stay in Iran and assuring them that American assistance would continue as planned. He was also to urge them to be loyal to Bakhtiar once he took power.

At the same time, the president sent a message to the shah through Sullivan. It supported the Bakhtiar government and pledged continuing American support for stability in Iran. It also approved the suggestion that the shah form a regency council and then leave Iran.

Sullivan met with the shah to inform him that "the United States government felt it was in his best interests and in Iran's for him to leave the country." In Sullivan's words: "The Shah listened to me state it as simply and gently as I could and then turned to me, almost beseeching, throwing out his hands and saying, 'Yes, but where will I go?' The cable of instruction had said nothing about this point. Accordingly, when the Shah asked this question I told him I had no guidance." The shah turned down both Switzerland (on security grounds) and Britain ("the weather is so bad"). "With that," Sullivan continues, "he sat there in silence, looking at me with soulful eyes. I then asked, 'Would you like me to seek an invitation for you to go to the United States?' He leaned forward, almost like a small boy, and said, 'Oh, would you?'"[79]

The US government quickly offered an invitation to the shah to stay in the country temporarily. At this point, Khomeini did not object: He and his associates were mainly concerned to speed the shah's departure, his destination being very much a secondary matter.

Sullivan followed up on this agreement with what he saw as "one final, rather impassioned effort to convince Washington to throw its weight behind a reconciliation between the military and the religious forces in Iran" in order to preempt a Communist effort to seize power.[80] The ambassador suggested that, when the shah reached the United States, President Carter should discourage any expectation that he would be returning to Iran by declaring an American commitment to such a reconciliation.

Several weeks earlier, with the shah's departure appearing imminent, Sullivan had (following his thoughts at the time of Azhari's heart attack) begun to act under the terms of his "thinking the unthinkable" telegram. In his words, "through telephone intercepts, we learned that [Mehdi] Bazargan and the Ayatollah Beheshti enjoyed the support of the Ayatollah Khomeini and would probably emerge as the leaders of the new government."[81] The Embassy had also learned, through direct talks with the opposition, that a number of senior officers "were not only sympathetic with the aims of the liberation movement but also closely in touch with its leaders on a regular basis."[82] The opposition actually supplied a list of some one hundred officers who would have to leave with the shah but, in doing so, it insisted that there would be no reprisals against those remaining. It was vital to know whether Khomeini himself would endorse this pledge. Further, Sullivan thought it critical that the nature of the transition to Bakhtiar be discussed with Khomeini before the shah departed.

Accordingly, by his testimony Sullivan proposed to Vance the sending of an emissary to Khomeini in France.[83] Vance and Sullivan agreed on terms of reference for such an emissary, and Vance chose for the task Theodore Eliot, the inspector-general of the Foreign Service, a former ambassador to Afghanistan, and a fluent Farsi linguist. A talking paper was developed, which stressed that the main concern of the United States was "the preservation of the territorial integrity of the country" and the maintenance of a strong and united military to ensure stability and territorial integrity. Eliot was to tell Khomeini "that [the US government] would be prepared to continue the military-assistance and sales programs currently in effect and that . . . a conflict between the Islamic forces and the Iranian military would benefit only the Soviet Union and their agents inside Iran."[84] January 6 was set as the date for the Eliot mission.

The White House first heard of the scheme on the eve of the president's departure for Guadeloupe on January 4 to attend a long-planned summit of Western leaders. Brzezinski, skeptical in any case, insisted that the plan be raised with the shah. Sullivan did as instructed; the shah listened "gravely and without enthusiasm" but voiced no objections. Vance called Carter in Guadeloupe, who consulted Brzezinski and then decided to postpone a decision until he returned to Washington. Sullivan, out on a perilous limb, recalled that his "anguish could not have been more complete" when he heard of the deferral. As he noted later, "at this point the frustrations that had beset me for so many months spilled over. I sent a short, sharp message to Secretary Vance saying that I thought the president had made a gross mistake and that a cancellation of the Eliot mission would be an irretrievable error."[85]

On January 10, in Washington, the president finally rejected the plan after passionate argument among his senior advisers. Sullivan then sent a passionate plea for reconsideration, calling the decision "insane," an "irretrievable" mistake. He had now reached the point of complete despair.[86]

Sullivan's response brought President Carter to the end of his patience. He asked Vance to "get Sullivan out of Iran." Vance convinced the president that changing ambassadors in mid-crisis would be a mistake, but Sullivan's credibility with the White House had come to an end. The United States had almost institutionalized two competing channels of communication to Iran.

When Sullivan went to the palace to pass on his bad news, the shah "became agitated. He asked why the mission had been canceled. I said I had received no information on that score. He then asked how we expected to influence these people if we would not even talk to them. He threw up his hands in despair and asked what we intended to do now. I had no answer."[87] The shah, as his own memoirs later made clear, had taken comfort in the belief that the United States had some kind of strategy for saving Iran from the opposition. At this point, he realized that this was an illusion.

Neither Sullivan nor the shah was entirely correct. Indeed, rightly or wrongly, Washington (or at least the NSC) had a firm, if questionable, view of what was happening and what might happen in Iran. On January 11, the mini-SCC met again to review developments. Taking notes, Sick felt a "remarkable consensus" developing around the table. The consensus was that Khomeini would not pose a great threat, for the National Front and other moderates in the opposition would actually lead the country. In any case, Khomeini probably would not make major changes and surely would not undo the popular portions of the shah's modernization. The obstacles to stability were the shah and Bakhtiar.[88]

Troubled by that easy consensus, Sick wrote a memo for Carter summarizing the meeting and attacking its conclusions. To Sick, the National Front seemed aging and divided. He believed Khomeini would create an Islamic republic that would "make the Shah look very good indeed by comparison."[89]

On January 11, Huyser reported to Defense Secretary Brown. His conversations had left him with the impression, that while the military wanted Bakhtiar to succeed, they had prepared contingency plans for a coup if he failed. Huyser's impressions were consistent with the line of policy in Washington, and they spurred Washington officialdom to refine options referred to as *A*, *B*, and *C*. *Plan A* was military support for the Bakhtiar government; *B* was military action to bolster it; and *C* was a military coup to replace it if public order collapsed.

Three days later, Huyser encouraged the Iranian military to establish contact with the religious leadership in order to clarify its intentions. By this time he estimated desertions from the military to be running at 500 to 1,000 per day. Those numbers, he reckoned, were tolerable in a force of 500,000, but they did reinforce the conviction of Khomeini and his colleagues that victory was near. One key colleague, Ayatollah Beheshti, told a US Embassy officer that he did not fear a confrontation with the military "since we control everyone below the rank of major."[90]

Also on the 14th, Carter authorized a meeting in Paris between Warren Zimmerman, the American political counselor there, and Ibrahim Yazdi, who had represented Khomeini in the United States.

EXERCISES

Set up two meetings, one consisting of US officials (including Zimmerman), the other of Khomeini, Yazdi, and one other aide to Khomeini. Each should develop (1) a brief opening statement for the Yazdi-Zimmerman meeting, and (2) a set of notes on aims, contingencies and conditions to guide the United States and Iranian opposition representatives respectively. Using the material thus provided, the students playing the roles of Yazdi and Zimmerman should then meet formally and alone, give their opening statements, and proceed to discuss the intentions, expectations, and requirements of the parties they represent. They should also seek clarification and further information on the aims and intentions of the other party. This meeting should be limited to 20-25 minutes. Once it has ended, the two representatives should draft a three-to-four-page report assessing the meeting and present it to their colleagues.

CONCLUSION

Zimmerman's meeting with Yazdi was in fact brief and amicable, mostly consisting of an exchange of prepared statements. Yazdi, citing coup rumors in Tehran, warned that if a coup occurred, Iranians would believe it was the work of the United States. For their part, Washingtonians, especially Brzezinski, were eager to see the "military option" remain alive, for they believed the threat of a coup would buy time for Bakhtiar to engineer a constitutional solution. Sullivan concurred and drafted language along those lines for Zimmerman's next meeting with Yazdi.

On January 16, the shah left Iran, this time, unlike 1953, not to return. His departure prompted noisy demonstrations in Iran. His first stop on his "well-deserved rest" was Anwar Sadat's Egypt. He then planned to go to the

United States, but ten days later changed his mind and accepted King Hassan's invitation to come to Morocco.

Zimmerman and Yazdi met again the same day. Huyser had reported that the Iranian military was extremely nervous about the possibility of Khomeini's return to Iran, fearing it would split the armed forces. Along the lines of his talking points, Zimmerman used the threat of a coup to forestall Khomeini's return. The military had discussed a coup, he told Yazdi, but had deferred to Huyser's urgings. However, if Khomeini were to return suddenly to Iran, the military's reaction would be unpredictable. Khomeini should neither return nor try to push the Bakhtiar government toward a collapse; rather, he should support the dialogue between the government and the religious leaders then being pursued in Tehran.

Yazdi said he knew of no plans for Khomeini's imminent return. He asked what the US meant by "protecting the constitution." The two men met three more times in the following week, ranging over US policy, the goals of the opposition, and relations between Iran and the United States, but to no more tangible result.

Large marches took place in Tehran without violence on the 19th, but the government was coming unglued. Bakhtiar said on the 20th that he would turn Iran over to the military if he could not consolidate his government, but the new chief of staff, General Gharabaghi, immediately threatened to resign lest he be part of a military takeover. Bakhtiar and Sullivan persuaded him to stay on. However, not only was the government further weakened, but the coup threat was becoming more and more threadbare. The next week, five air force personnel were arrested after taking part in a pro-Khomeini demonstration in Tehran.

When Zimmerman and Yazdi met for the last time on the 27th, Yazdi delivered the first personal message from Khomeini to Washington. It said that the actions of Bakhtiar and the senior Iranian military were damaging Iran, the US government, and the future of Americans in Iran, and it threatened "new orders" bringing "great disaster" if the state of affairs continued.

Bakhtiar proposed to meet with Khomeini in Paris to discuss a constitutional solution, but Khomeini replied that he would attend only if Bakhtiar first resigned.[91] Khomeini would then appoint him to the provisional government. Talks between representatives of the two men broke off after two days, and Bakhtiar said that he would not go to Paris. However, he also announced that Iranian airports would be opened for Khomeini's return.

Khomeini flew from Paris to Tehran on February 1, ending fourteen years of exile. He received a tumultuous greeting from over a million people, and immediately took up residence in a small Tehran school building. Soon after arriving, he rejected a plan worked out between Bakhtiar and Bazargan for a popular referendum offering a choice between the monarchy and an Islamic republic. Khomeini continued to insist that Bakhtiar resign first, regarding both him and the regency council as creatures of the shah, and therefore illegal.

Huyser returned to the United States on February 3, having become a target for the opposition. In briefing the president and other senior officials, Huyser painted a bleak picture: Iran, he reported, was unstable, and a Khomeini takeover would bring a catastrophe--a drift to the left and an eventual communist takeover.[92] About what to do the president's advisers remained divided again, particularly over the role of the military. Huyser felt the military should clearly support the Bakhtiar government until a new constitution was written, while Sullivan thought it better for the military to step aside while the political groups contended.[93] He thought the political outcome would be an Islamic republic that was democratically inclined.

The continuing division between his advisers distressed President Carter. He was even more upset by indications that Sullivan had not been carrying out his instructions, many of which had been drafted personally by Vance and Carter. The final straw for the president came when, after the Huyser meeting, a *Washington Post* story quoted "State Department officials" who did not expect the Bakhtiar government to last more than a few days.[94] Carter angrily called in the senior officials of the State Department and (in his own words) "laid down the law to them as strongly as I knew how."[95] He told them to resign if they could not support his decisions, and he threatened firings if the leaks continued.

Washington remained in contact with the Iranian military after Huyser left through General Philip Gast, chief of the Military Assistance and Advisory Group in Tehran. Gast, like Huyser, reported to Brown daily on the secure phone. On the 9th he reported fighting between air force *homafars* (civilian technicians whom the shah's government had forced to stay in low-paying jobs after their contracts expired) and imperial guards at an airbase on the outskirts of Tehran, touched off by a television broadcast of Khomeini's return. The fighting was quelled within hours but broke out again the next morning. A curfew was imposed on Tehran as demonstrations and fires spread throughout the city.

In Washington, Brzezinski convened an emergency session of the SCC on the morning of February 11 to assess American influence over events and the future safety of Americans still in Iran. American influence seemed to be rapidly approaching zero. Reports from Tehran indicated that Bakhtiar's whereabouts were unknown and that the military had withdrawn to its barracks. Though everyone at the meeting believed the military would not act, Brzezinski insisted that support for a coup be presented as an option to the president. "If the military had the will and the capacity to take control of the situation," Brzezinski later wrote, "we should [have been] prepared to act like a major power and support them."[96]

When Carter called from Camp David, Brzezinski discussed the military option (option *C*) with him. As they spoke a call came in from Huyser, who said option *C* would not work without a major American commitment. From Tehran, Sullivan reported that the military was in the process of making an accommodation with Bazargan and could not be counted on. Reluctantly, Brzezinski concluded that the military option was dead: "It was clear to me," he wrote later, "that we were faced with a fait accompli."[97]

That same day, February 11, Bakhtiar and the members of the Majlis (parliament) resigned. With Khomeini's backing, power passed to Bazargan, the man whom Sullivan had earlier predicted would be the first leader to emerge from the revolution. The fall of the shah was complete, though the agony for the United States was far from over.

DISCUSSION QUESTIONS

1. *Was the outcome of the Iranian crisis a "failure" for US foreign policy, as widely claimed at the time?*
2. *What kind of failure was it (or what/who was it that failed)?*
3. *What were the goals of US foreign policy relative to Iran and to this crisis? To what extent were they advanced or undermined by the outcome of the crisis and by the way in which it was handled?*
4. *To what extent did the actions of the US administration actually contribute to the course and outcome of the crisis?*
5. *What did the crisis reveal about the character and limits of American power?*
6. *What special difficulties did the Iranian problem present compared to the others of a broadly similar kind described in this book?*

NOTES

1. The text in this section is adapted from Steigman, 2.
2. *Ibid.*

3. *Ibid.*

4. Sir Anthony Parsons, *The Pride and the Fall. Iran 1974-1979* (London: Jonathan Cape, 1984), 7.

5. This section is adapted from Steigman, *The Iranian Hostage Negotiations*, 2.

6. Nixon and the shah had known each other each other as far back as 1953 when, as vice-president, Nixon had visited the shah after the CIA-sponsored coup that restored his authority.

7. This section adapted from Steigman, *Iranian Hostage Negotiations*, 2.

8. Henry Kissinger, *White House Years* (Boston: Little, Brown, 1979), 1262.

9. Gregory Treverton and James Klocke, interview with Henry Precht, October 24, 1986. Foreign officials who spoke fluent Farsi were regarded with suspicion by the Iranian government (and in some cases by the opposition). A British officer sent to Iran to help commission tanks for the Iranian army was declared *persona non grata*, apparently because of his fluency.

10. Gary Sick, *All Fall Down* (New York: Penguin, 1986), 24.

11. *Ibid.*, 25.

12. The text in this section is adapted from Steigman, *The Iranian Hostage Negotiations*, 3.

13. *Ibid.*

14. *Ibid.*

15. Parsons, *The Pride and the Fall*, 16.

16. *Ibid.*, 19.

17. The text in this section is adapted from Steigman, *The Iranian Hostage Negotiations*, 3.

18. Both citations in this paragraph are from *Ibid.*, 4.

19. *US News and World Report*, June 26, 1978, 37.

20. Parsons, *The Pride and the Fall*, 63.

21. *Ibid.*, 66.

22. John D. Stempel, *Inside the Iranian Revolution* (Bloomington: Indiana University Press, 1981), 138.

23. Gregory Treverton and James Klocke, interview with Henry Precht, October 24, 1986.

24. William H. Sullivan, *Mission to Iran* (New York: W. W. Norton, 1981), 55, 57.

25. Parsons, *The Pride and the Fall*, 74.

26. *Ibid.*, 74.

27. According to Stempel, the Shah rejected several proposals for the assassination of Khomeini: three intelligence services (not including the CIA) allegedly suggested assassination (Stempel, *Inside the Iranian Revolution*, 125).

28. Sick, *All Fall Down*, 69.

29. Cited in *Ibid.*, 70.

30. *Ibid.*

31. Doubts which, according to Stempel, were increasingly shared by the shah's own inner circle and other members of the elite, many of whom began to wonder "whether their ruler was as shrewd a politician as his historical reputation suggested" (Stempel, *Inside the Iranian Revolution*, 125). Their disenchantment was strengthened by the shah's tendency to sacrifice unpopular but loyal officials in order to propitiate the opposition.

32. Parsons, *The Pride and the Fall*, 82-83.

33. *Ibid.*, 85.

34. Zbigniew Brzezinski, *Power and Principle: Memoirs of the National Security Adviser* (New York: Farrar, Straus, Giroux, 1983), 355.

35. Ambassador Sullivan noted, "The Shah would regularly speak to me about Zahedi's activities and tell me he did not approve of them. . . . He asked me to inform Washington that Zahedi did not understand the domestic situation in Iran and that, although his heart was in the right place, he was out of touch with reality" (Sullivan, *Mission to Iran*, 193).

36. *Ibid.*, 171-172.

37. *Ibid.*

38. Parsons, *The Pride and the Fall*, 90-91.

39. *Ibid.*, 91.

40. Sick, *All Fall Down*, 104.

41. Brzezinski in fact sent a directive requesting a joint State/CIA review of US political reporting on Iran and at the same time sent a memo to Carter complaining about the quality of political intelligence more generally. On November 11, Carter sent a handwritten note to Vance, Brzezinski, and Turner, directing them to improve political intelligence capabilities. The note was leaked to the press, embarrassing the administration and turning the government's debate over the quality of its intelligence into a public one.

42. Sullivan, *Mission to Iran*, 193.

43. The shah reportedly remarked in mid-November: "If I can't be commander-in-chief I'll pack my bags and leave." His refusal to concede control of the armed forces created a problem for opposition leaders trying to get Khomeini to agree to a negotiated settlement with the shah. The ayatollah could always argue that as long as the shah could use the military to overturn a civilian government, there was no point in easing the pressure on him, much less cooperating with him (Stempel, *Inside the Iranian Revolution*, 149).

44. Sullivan, *Mission to Iran*, 190.

45. For Sullivan's account of this message, see his "Dateline Iran: The Road Not Taken," *Foreign Policy* 40, Fall 1980, 179-180, and *Mission to Iran*, 201-203.

46. Sullivan, *Mission to Iran*, 181.

47. On negotiations that occurred during November between the US Embassy's political section and the Liberation Front (a group close to the fundamentalists and led by Mehdi Bazargan, among others) and between the Embassy and Ayatollah Beheshti, an associate of Khomeini, Sullivan observed

that both were "generally well-disposed toward the United States." He added, "They seemed to recognize that the prime threat to the future of Iran came from the Soviet Union and that the United States, despite its close association with the shah, had long been a force for social, economic and political improvement for the people of Iran (*Ibid.*, 200).

48. *Ibid.*, 202. Both Sick and Brzezinski, in their synopses of Sullivan's cable, note that the ambassador predicted that Khomeini would occupy a "Gandhi-like" role once an accommodation was reached between the younger military officers and the moderate religious leaders. Sullivan himself does not (understandably enough) quote this phrase. Brzezinski described Sullivan's scenario for a "moderate" succession as a "Pollyanna prospect" (*Power and Principle*, 368). In fairness, it should be noted that several observers (for example, the scholar James Bill) forecast that the moderate opposition would prevail, that the mullahs "would never participate directly in the formal governmental structure," and that "a future government in Iran would not necessarily be antithetical to American interests" (James Bill, "Iran and the Crisis of '78," *Foreign Affairs*, Winter 1978/79, quoted in Sick, *All Fall Down*, 131-132).

49. Sullivan, *Mission to Iran*, 202-203. Sullivan's evident preoccupation with a Soviet threat to Iran was shared by Brzezinski whose approach to the crisis was determined by geopolitical considerations. It was not (as noted in the text) shared by his British colleague, Sir Anthony Parsons, or by his own political officer, John D. Stempel, who later noted in his history of the Iranian revolution: "Soviet propaganda remained neutral towards the Shah. There is no evidence of significant additional Russian involvement with the various dissident factions, only indirect military aid to guerrilla groups, channeled through the PLO for a decade, and the traditional modest financial assistance to the Tudeh Party" (*Inside the Iranian Revolution*, 138). Stempel goes on to suggest that the course of the revolution was in all important respects impervious (not to mention incomprehensible) to foreigners and their influence: "No foreign nation significantly affected the Iranian policy and decision making process, which remained mysterious and secretive to the man on the street and confused and complex to those involved" (138).

50. Sick, *All Fall Down*, 96.

51. Sullivan, *Mission to Iran*, 191.

52. "I waited in vain for any such response. We drifted through the remainder of November and into December with no guidance from the Department of State or from Washington in general" (*Ibid.*, 204).

53. Sullivan, *Mission to Iran*, 206.

54. Writing of Sullivan's November 2 cable warning of the shah's remarks about possible abdication, Brzezinski commented: "Without prior warning and contrary to his earlier assessments, the Ambassador requested guidance within forty-eight hours.... Since Ambassador Sullivan had not requested guidance until now, his cable convinced me that we had reached a crisis stage (*Power and Principle*, 359).

55. *Ibid.*, 359, 367. According to Brzezinski, Sullivan, like his predecessors, had restricted Embassy contact with the opposition as a whole.

56. Sick, *All Fall Down*, 202-203.

57. *Ibid.*, 101. Brzezinski comments that the cable, "while carefully neither predicting nor advocating the Shah's resignation, did have the effect of strengthening the views of those in the State Department who were generally inclined to argue that the fall of the Shah would have benign consequences for American interests" (*Power and Principle*, 368).

58. Cited in Gregory Treverton and James Klocke, *The Fall of the Shah of Iran* (Pew case no. 311), 10.

59. Quoted in *Ibid.*, 19.

60. Sick, *All Fall Down*, 83.

61. George Ball, *The Past Has Another Pattern* (New York: Norton, 1982), 456. Brzezinski initially approved of Blumenthal's suggestion, but afterwards "came to regret" his approval.

62. Sick, *All Fall Down*, 121.

63. Quoted in *Ibid.*, 128.

64. Ball, *The Past Has Another Pattern*, 457.

65. Sullivan was pleased by the appointment of Ball, whose views on Iran he regarded as "sound." He hoped that Ball would "consolidate what appeared to be an increasingly shattered administration effort to find some common policy" (*Mission to Iran*, 220). However, Sullivan didn't see the eventual Ball report, and he didn't agree with its recommendation of a council of elders.

66. Ball, *The Past Has Another Pattern*, 458-462.

67. Brzezinski, *Power and Principle*, 370.

68. *Ibid.*, 370-371. Sick notes, somewhat gleefully, that Brzezinski was "hoist on his own petard." Having brought Ball in, Brzezinski "now found himself for the first time in the crisis confronted with a vigorous and articulate opponent with sufficient stature to carry his views directly to the president (Sick, *All Fall Down*, 409, n.4).

69. Quoted in Sick, *All Fall Down*, 136.

70. In his memoirs, Ball notes that he told President Carter that the notion of sending Brzezinski was "with all due respect . . . the worst idea I have ever heard" (*The Past Has Another Pattern*, 461).

71. *Ibid.*, 462.

72. Quoted in Sick, *All Fall Down*, 141.

73. In Tehran, Sullivan was called suddenly to see Azhari on his sickbed. The Prime Minister insisted on talking about the political situation, telling the ambassador that the armed forces were tired and demoralized. Then, in Sullivan's words, Azhari "propped himself up on one elbow and, looking at me, said, 'You must know this and you must tell it to your government. This country is lost because the king cannot make up his mind.' With that he settled back on his pillow. We shook hands and I left" (*Mission to Iran*, 212).

74. Sick, *All Fall Down*, 140.

75. Sullivan, *Mission to Iran*, 212.

76. Sullivan noted that whenever he met Bakhtiar, he found it hard to believe that he was talking to an Iranian: "An habitue of the French Club in Tehran . . . Bakhtiar was one of the most complete Francophiles I have ever encountered. He spoke exclusively in French, dressed in French-tailored clothes, he had French mannerisms, and he even looked like a French country gentleman (*Ibid.*, 213, 235).

77. Indeed, the shah "outlined all [Bakhtiar's] weaknesses and then told me he was 'one of those worms' that always crawls out of the woodwork in times of trouble" (*Ibid.*, 213).

78. *Ibid.*, 235.

79. *Ibid.*, 230-231.

80. *Ibid.*, 233.

81. Quoted in Treverton and Klocke, *The Fall of the Shah of Iran*, 15.

82. Sullivan, *Mission to Iran*, 221.

83. The discussion took place on the secure telephone, Sullivan fearing that any classified cables he sent would, if the NSC staff disagreed with them, "appear, almost verbatim, in *New York Times*" (Sullivan, "Dateline Iran," 181).

84. Sullivan, *Mission to Iran*, 222, 223.

85. *Ibid.*, 224.

86. "As far as I could see," Sullivan wrote, "the United States was facing the situation in Iran with no policy whatsoever. The Shah's collapse, in my judgment, was inevitable, and unless some understanding were reached for an accommodation between the armed forces and the Islamic forces, I felt that an explosion would occur" (*Ibid.*, 225).

87. *Ibid.*, 226.

88. Sick, *All Fall Down*, 162.

89. *Ibid.*, 162.

90. Quoted in *Ibid.*, 164.

91. Sullivan found Bakhtiar's approach to the political situation "quixotic." He listened with "considerable disbelief" as Bakhtiar talked "of going to Paris to meet with the ayatollah and making arrangements for the latter to have an honorific religious position outside the realm of government, while he, Bakhtiar, organized the political functions of the state" (*Mission to Iran*, 235-235). Sullivan told Washington that Bakhtiar would be swept aside by the revolution. In reply, he was told that the US government's position was still one of support for the Bakhtiar government.

92. Jimmy Carter, *Keeping Faith: Memoirs of a President* (New York: Bantam Books, 1982), 449.

93. Sullivan describes the conversations that took place every evening at the Embassy in Tehran between himself and Huyser. Sullivan thought that the Iranian military had lost its will and would be split across family lines if conflict occurred between it and the Muslim fundamentalists. He therefore advocated promoting talks between the heads of the armed forces and Bazar-

gan and Khomeini's representatives. Huyser (in Sullivan's words) "heard me out and respected my judgment, but his own conclusions were to the contrary." Huyser believed that the military was prepared to act against Khomeini, and after the Shah's departure he sensed that they were becoming more prepared to support Bakhtiar (*Mission to Iran*, 238).

94. Sick, *All Fall Down*, 180.
95. Carter, *Keeping Faith*, 449.
96. Brzezinski, *Power and Principle*, 391.
97. *Ibid.*, 393.

FURTHER READING ON IRAN

Books

Bill, James A. *The Eagle and the Lion: The Tragedy of American-Iranian Relations*. New Haven, CT: Yale University Press, 1988.

Bill, James A. *The Shah, the Ayatollah and the US*. New York: Foreign Policy Association, 1988. Headline Series pamphlet no. 285 (excerpts from above).

Brzezinski, Zbigniew. *Power and Principle. Memoirs of the National Security Adviser, 1977-1981*. New York: Farrar, Straus, Giroux, 1983 (especially Chapter 10, "The Fall of the Shah").

Cottam, Richard W. *Nationalism in Iran*. Pittsburgh: University of Pittsburgh Press, 1978.

Keddie, Nikki R. *Roots of Revolution: An Interpretive History of Modern Iran*. New Haven, CT: Yale University Press, 1981.

Ledeen, Michael and William Lewis. *Debacle: The American Failure in Iran*. New York: Alfred A. Knopf, 1981.

Pahlavi, Mohammad Reza. *Answer to History*. New York: Stein and Day, 1980.

Parsons, Sir Anthony. *The Pride and the Fall. Iran 1974-1979*. London: Jonathan Cape, 1984.

Ramazani, R.K. *Revolutionary Iran: Challenge and Response in the Middle East*. Baltimore: Johns Hopkins University Press, 1987.

Rubin, Barry M. *Paved with Good Intentions: The American Experience and Iran*. New York: Oxford University Press, 1987.

Saikal, Amin. *The Rise and Fall of the Shah*. Princeton, NJ: Princeton University Press, 1980.

Sick, Gary. *All Fall Down. America's Tragic Encounter with Iran*. New York: Penguin, 1986.

Stempel, John D. *Inside the Iranian Revolution*. Bloomington: Indiana University Press, 1981.

Sullivan, William H. *Mission to Iran*. New York: W. W. Norton, 1981.

Articles

Bill, James A. "Iran and the Crisis of '78." *Foreign Affairs* 57, 2 (Winter 1978-79): 323-342.

Ledeen, Michael, and William Lewis. "Carter and the Fall of the Shah: The Inside Story." *Washington Quarterly* 3 (1980): 3-40.

Nickel, Herman. "The US Failure in Iran." *Fortune* 12 (March 1979): 106.

Sullivan, William H. "Dateline Iran: The Road Not Taken," *Foreign Policy* 40 (Fall 1980): 175-186.

5

THE PHILIPPINES, 1985–1986
The Fall of Ferdinand E. Marcos

Compared to the fall of the shah of Iran, the removal of President Ferdinand E. Marcos of the Philippines in 1985-1986 was widely greeted as a success for US policy. Alone of the cases presented here, the transition brought in a government acceptable to the United States, partly because Washington had begun the process of distancing itself from the incumbent fairly early and had openly and covertly helped the opposition.

Yet the "success" was paradoxical in some respects. It occurred under the Reagan administration, which was more committed to supporting "friends" with orthodox anti-Communist credentials than its predecessor. Indeed, a distinctive feature of the case is that the predictable division among policy-makers ran not between or within agencies, or even between the NSC and the State Department, but between, on the one hand, a broad group of officials and elected members who were agreed on the imminence and the desirability of Marcos's removal from power and, on the other, the president and his personal entourage who remained loyal to Marcos until the last moment. The case is a particularly good illustration of the process by which a consensus grows and of a way that a "policy network" develops around an issue. It also illustrates vividly the highly personal character both of the relationships

---

This chapter is primarily the work of William E. Kline as presented in his case study, The Fall of Marcos, *Pew case study no. 439, with additional material inserted by the editor from Donald M. Goldstein,* US Policy Concerning Renewal of the Military Base Agreement with the Philippines *(Pew case study no. 325) and from other cases and secondary sources as indicated in the notes.*

created by links between patrons and clients and of the diplomacy involved in changing or ending them.

A further question relates to the true reasons for "success" in this case. Was the Reagan administration's handling of the problem truly superior to the Carter administration's performance in the Nicaraguan and Iranian crises? Or was its "success" partly or largely a matter of luck--in that it found itself dealing at once with a dictator that few, even in the White House, truly respected and with an opposition whom few, even in the White House, could fail to admire?

* * *

On August 21, 1983, Benigno Aquino, the main political rival of President Ferdinand Marcos of the Philippines, was returning by air to his country after three years in exile. Warned by several Filipinos (including Mrs. Imelda Marcos) of possible plots to assassinate him, Aquino put on a bulletproof vest as his plane descended toward Manila. Shortly after landing, Aquino was escorted from the plane by three uniformed Philippine soldiers. All the other passengers were made to remain in their seats. Seconds after Aquino left the plane, shots rang out. By the time the press could get to the scene, Aquino's body and that of his alleged assassin lay on the tarmac near the stairway leading from the aircraft door. Aquino had been shot in the back of the head at close range.

The assassination of Aquino (like that of Pedro Joaquin Chamorro in Nicaragua) marked the beginning of another crisis for an apparently well-entrenched ally of the United States. But this crisis had an outcome significantly different from the others examined in this book.

THE STATUS QUO

Filipino contact with the West began in 1521 when Ferdinand Magellan claimed the islands for Spain. Spanish colonial government lasted from 1565 until 1898 and left a population largely converted to Roman Catholicism (currently, 80 percent of Filipinos are Catholics).

A rebellion against colonial rule in the 1890s culminated in 1898 in an attack on the Spanish garrison in Manila by forces led by Emilio Aguinaldo. The United States gave moral support to the rebels, and in May 1898 Commodore Dewey defeated an aging Spanish fleet in Manila harbor.

However, cooperation between the Americans and the Filipino nationalists quickly broke down. Although Aguinaldo's men already controlled many of the islands and were intent on setting up an independent republic, the United States saw the Philippines as strategically useful for protecting trade routes to China.[1] The United States and Spain therefore struck a deal that provided for direct surrender of the islands to US forces in August 1898, Aguinaldo's forces being excluded from the agreement. The transfer (along with that of Guam and Puerto Rico) was formalized in the Treaty of Paris in December 1898.[2]

In a subsequent war between the United States and Aguinaldo's army, over 4,000 Americans and some 200,000 Filipinos were killed. From 1899 until 1934, the Philippines were directly governed by the United States under a policy of "benevolent assimilation," which brought significant developments in public education, administration, and commerce (the Philippines enjoying preferential access to US markets).

In 1934, the Americans passed the Tydings-McDuffie Act, which granted the islands commonwealth status and gave the Filipinos self-government in all areas except foreign policy. Over the course of the next few years, the Philippine government drafted its own constitution, built up a system of national defense, and elected a president, Manuel Quezon, a former officer in Aguinaldo's army. Under the provisions of the Tydings-McDuffie Act, the islands were to be granted full independence after a ten-year transition period under the new government. During this era, much of the ill feeling left by the circumstances of American rule began to evaporate, largely due to the Philippine conviction that the Americans intended to make good on the promise of independence for the islands.[3]

Indeed, the United States did intend to grant the islands their independence in 1946 as promised. From both an economic and military viewpoint, the Americans had little reason not to do so. Trade with the region had not developed at the rate economists had predicted at the beginning of the century, and the United States had few vital security interests in the area. Until this time, American military bases in the Philippines had mainly been important as a means to check growing Japanese power in the Pacific.[4] Therefore, if the islanders could demonstrate an ability to manage their own affairs by 1946, the United States saw no reason why they should not let the Filipinos have their independence.[5]

On December 8, 1941, however, the Japanese attacked the Philippines, driving out the small American force commanded by General Douglas MacArthur. A long struggle ensued, culminating in the landing of MacArthur and American troops on Leyte in October 1944. More than one million Filipinos were killed during the war, and the country was devastated.[6]

The Philippines finally became independent on July 4, 1946. But independence did not bring an end to armed struggle in the islands. During the Japanese occupation, the Philippine Communist and Socialist parties and a number of peasant organizations joined to form the Hukbalahaps, or Huks, who fought a guerrilla war against the Japanese. When the Huks were not given a role in the postindependence government, they returned to guerrilla warfare. Despite their program of reforming peasant land tenure, the Huks enjoyed only limited popular support, and after reaching a peak of some 11,000-15,000 armed troops between 1949-1951, the movement fizzled out and died during the tenure of the popular Ramon Magsaysay, who served as Philippine president from 1953 until his death in 1957.[7]

US Interests in the Philippines

American interests in the Philippines during the Cold War years were strategic, diplomatic, and economic. The latter were initially secured by the law granting independence, which included preferential trade arrangements between the United States and the Philippines. By the same law, Americans were given equal rights with Filipinos in exploiting the country's agricultural and mineral resources and in owning and operating public utilities. The latter caused great resentment among Filipino nationalists and was eventually revoked, although some of the provisions granting preferential trade to Americans were in effect until 1974. In 1985, some $2 billion of American capital remained as direct investments in the Philippines, while total annual trade stood at about $4 billion. About half of the Philippines foreign debt, which ran to approximately $26 billion, was owed to US banks.

Much more prominent in official thinking (both American and Filipino) was the question of American military bases. In 1947, the United States and the Philippines signed a Military Bases Agreement that allowed the Americans to retain rights to twenty-three military installations in the Philippines for a rent-free period of some ninety-nine years. The bases, which included the extensive naval installations at Subic Bay as well as Clark Air Base, were to remain under the full jurisdiction of the Americans during that period.[8]

Also in 1947, the United States and the Philippines signed a second treaty affecting their security relationship. This one, the Military Assistance Agreement, was much more along the lines of what the Philippines had hoped to get from their former colonial ruler. It provided for the creation of a Joint United States Military Advisory Group (JUSMAG), which would advise and train the inexperienced Philippine armed forces, and earmarked economic and material aid to the islands to the tune of $169 million over the next ten years. [9] Such assistance was valuable to the Philippine government for both development and security purposes (as long as the Huk insurgency posed a threat).

In 1952, a third, and from the Filipino viewpoint most valuable, agreement was concluded. The 1952 bilateral Mutual Defense Treaty found the United States at the height of its Cold War containment mood, and seizing the moment, the Filipinos were able to secure an American commitment for assistance in the event of an armed attack against their borders. Without question, this era marked the high point in the security relationship between the United States and the Philippines, and perhaps the only time in their histories that both countries have seen eye to eye on the need for American bases on the islands.[10]

For the United States, the bases (especially Clark Air Base and Subic Bay Naval Base) were crucial to its Pacific strategy of containment. Clark became the headquarters for the Thirteenth Air Force, which was (and is) responsible for air operations in the Western Pacific. Subic Bay was the largest US naval installation outside the United States, able to support carrier battle groups and provide supplies for operations by the US Seventh Fleet in the Pacific and Indian Oceans. Together, the bases provided the ideal staging point for Cold War operations throughout Southeast Asia, including Korea, Vietnam, and the Philippines itself.[11]

Both major bases were used to support operations during the Vietnam War, although no US combat missions were flown from the Philippines because of Philippine objections. Strategically, they enabled the United States to protect sea lanes crucial for the movement of oil supplies to Japan and South Korea, as well as to provide military assistance to those countries.[12] They were also considered useful for supporting possible operations in the Persian Gulf. At least until the late 1980s, the bases were considered indispensable by American officials and politicians, even those otherwise critical of US policy in the region.[13]

For the Filipinos, the bases provided assurances of American military and economic assistance in their effort to defend against both internal and external Communist threats, as well as a significant source of income to improve their economic condition. Nevertheless, they represented to critics an infringement of sovereignty, and resentment on this score began to grow during the 1960s. A major Philippine grievance was the exceedingly generous terms of the 1947 agreement with regard to the length of the lease. Following negotiations in 1965 and 1966, the lease was shortened to 25 years (1966-1991). According to this amendment, in 1991 the treaty would become subject to abrogation by either party upon one year's notice, provided that it was not renewed or otherwise extended.[14]

Despite such tension over the bases, the United States and the Philippines were in essential agreement on foreign policy. As one scholar wrote in 1985: "During the first two decades after the Philippines became independent in 1946, the foreign policy of the republic could be defined in terms of a simple formula: a close alignment with the policies of the United States on the assumption that the fundamental objectives of the two countries, in domestic as well as international affairs, were essentially identical."[15] One clear expression of this relationship was the signing of the Manila Treaty in September 1954, which created the American-led Southeast Asia Treaty Organization (SEATO). In response to the French withdrawal from Vietnam, the United States was able to convince seven nations, including the Philippines, to pledge their assistance in the effort to prevent the advance of the North Vietnamese Communist forces into South Vietnam and other adjacent areas.[16]

On the economic front, the United States and the Philippines struck yet another agreement during this period in the form of the Laurel-Langley Agreement of 1955, which provided the two nations with a means to regulate their trade relations over the next twenty years.[17] Continuing the policy of his predecessors, in 1966 President Marcos helped form the Association of Southeast Asian Nations (ASEAN), a coalition of five nations designed to foster better economic, political, and security relations between its members.[18] Marcos, however, resisted American pressure to send troops to Vietnam, eventually sending only an engineering battalion of 2,000.

The Marcos Regime

Ferdinand E. Marcos, a native of Ilocos Norte in the northern Philippines, came from a relatively comfortable and politically well-connected family background. He showed evidence of political ambition and a great capacity for hard work from a very early age. His personal advancement was, however, interrupted in 1941 by the Japanese invasion, against which he fought though not as heroically or for as long as he subsequently claimed.[19]

After the war, Marcos launched himself into an intensely competitive political career, being elected to the House of Representatives at the age of 32. In 1954, he married Imelda Romualdez, a poor member of a politically powerful family, a former girlfriend of Benigno Aquino, and an ex-beauty queen. Together, Marcos and his wife built up a political following, at the core of which were fellow Ilocanos (such as his cousin Fabian Ver, successively Marcos's chauffeur, commander of the palace guard, and chief of staff of the Philippine armed forces). After being elected to the Senate in 1959, Marcos became its president and in 1965, in a particularly gruelling and corrupt campaign, he led the Nationalist party ticket to become president of the Philippines, beating the incumbent Liberal, Diosdado Macapagal. Under different circumstances and constitutional provisions, Marcos was reelected president in 1969, ruled under martial law from 1972 to 1980, and was again reelected in 1981.

In maintaining his hold on power, Marcos permitted no real political opposition to develop. Nevertheless, opposition organizations were created and did survive. Two were engaged in armed struggle against the government. On the Marxist left was the New People's Army (NPA), the military wing of the outlawed Communist party of the Philippines (CPP). The NPA was set up in 1968 in Tarlac Province by Bernabe Buscayno, a dedicated Maoist and a firm advocate of the strategy of "People's Democratic Revolution." Over the course of the next few years, Buscayno's popularity grew with some of the more radical student organizations at the University of Manila, who were attracted by the NPA's disdain for the ruling Filipino elite and its condemnation of the "imperialistic" American military presence. By the early 1970s, the NPA's ranks were growing, and the rebels had taken control of much of the northeast coast of the island of Luzon.

Quite different, but equally threatening to Marcos, was the Moro National Liberation Front (MNLF), which represented 33 percent of the population of Mindanao in their struggle against the dominant Christians. The MNLF launched a rebellion against the Marcos government in 1969, demanding self-determination for Mindanao, the Sulu Archipelago, and Palawan. It was supported in its campaign by Malaysia and several Middle Eastern nations, including Libya.

Marcos also had to face opposition in the urban areas of the Philippines from labor unions and students, with some encouragement by the CPP. As he moved to crack down on the opposition, a cycle of violence between Philippine police and protesters developed. Finally, in 1972, rioting in front of the US Embassy, an attempt on the life of visiting Pope Paul VI, an attempt on the life of Defense Minister Juan Ponce Enrile, and an effort by demonstrators to storm Marcos's residence led the president to declare martial law. US officials generally supported Marcos's claim that the move was necessary to avert a leftist overthrow of the government. Back in Manila, however, the president and his wife had seen that the situation presented an opportunity for them to do far more than just fend off the attacks of a few leftist student organizations.

Marcos was now convinced that it was his destiny to transform the Philippines into a "New Society" under his leadership. With the writ of habeas corpus suspended and the armed forces at his disposal, he set about eliminating his political opposition through a combined system of arrests, kidnappings, and murders. Among those arrested was Benigno Aquino, at this time a senator, leader of the Liberal party, and the probable opposition candidate in the 1973 presidential election. Shortly after proclaiming martial law, Marcos had Aquino and many other political opponents arrested, and Aquino spent the next eight years in detention. A military tribunal convicted him of providing arms to Communist guerrillas and plotting the murder of a local politician. Aquino was sentenced to death in November 1977, but in May 1980 Marcos commuted the sentence and allowed Aquino to go to the United States for medical treatment.

Under martial law, Marcos set out to propagate a new philosophy expressing his vision of a New Society. In establishing a new political party, the KBL, he announced that he was pioneering "a third world approach to democracy," that he would take the lead in land reform, and that he would create citizen assemblies in order to "restore power to the people."[20] Marcos had a new constitution approved that allowed him to continue as president; he also began to consolidate his power by centralizing governmental authority until all major policy decisions were controlled by him and his network of political and military cronies. He closed down the Philippine Congress, assumed its legislative authorities, and issued over one thousand presidential decrees, which were considered law, by 1976 alone. Taking advantage of the nationalism stirred up by his opponents, he declared that in future his foreign policy would involve seeking "a rendezvous with Asia"--a phrase that implied fewer rendezvous with Washington.

Yet despite the distaste that some American officials felt for Marcos and his wife--for their ostentation and evident corruption--official relations between the United States and Marcos remained cordial. Like Anastasio Somoza, the Filipino president specialized in befriending American politicians, especially Republicans. In 1969 Governor Ronald Reagan attended the opening of a cultural center in Manila as President Nixon's special representative. From that point on, the Marcoses felt they had a special personal relationship with the Reagans; Nancy Reagan is reported to have felt the same way. President Nixon himself paid a visit to Manila in 1969, as did President Ford in 1975.

The Carter Administration

With the Democrats, particularly President Carter, Marcos had a harder time, finding himself openly criticized for abuse of human rights. However, Carter, like other American presidents, had to weigh the value of the Philippine bases against any concern he might have about the regime in Manila. Indeed, the Carter administration's alarm about Soviet intentions put Marcos in a unusually good bargaining position with the Americans. He used his advantage with great skill in negotiations over the bases, negotiations that began under President Ford but were resumed in 1977 at the initiative of Richard Holbrooke, Carter's assistant secretary of state for East Asian and Pacific affairs. Knowing that President Carter could not afford to lose his most valuable strategic asset in Asia, Marcos paid little heed to the American president's threats to cut aid if political reforms were not forthcoming from Manila. Instead, he began to circulate rumors to the effect that the Filipinos would seek aid from Moscow if there were none to be found in Washington. He noted that this naturally would have serious ramifications for the upcoming base talks. With this ace in hand, Marcos was able to secure very favorable terms for the Philippines in the 1978 negotiations, including the reaffirmation of Philippine sovereignty over the bases, and a $500 million, five-year military and economic assistance package from the Americans. In addition, he convinced the United States to accept a stipulation calling for a review of the terms of the agreement every five years until its termination. This review was to include a reassessment of the objectives, provisions, and duration of the agreement by both parties. For their part, the Americans were able to secure continued, unhampered access to the bases, and it was agreed that US authorities would retain jurisdiction over all American personnel, equipment, and materials on the bases.

The Reagan Administration

After his troubles with the Carter administration, Marcos was relieved by the election of Ronald Reagan as president in 1980. He quickly moved to lift martial law, partly because of continuing criticism from the Roman Catholic Church led by Cardinal Jaime Sin and partly to remove any obstacles to his relationship with Washington. But in abolishing martial law, Marcos also had the Philippine constitution amended so as to strengthen the presidency. Under these amendments, the presidential term was lengthened from four to six years, existing limits on the number of terms an individual might serve were removed, and an incumbent president was even given the right to nominate his successor.[21]

In June 1981 Marcos was elected to a six-year term, winning some 86 percent of the vote. His victory was capped by the attendance of Vice-President Bush at his inauguration, an occasion marked by Bush's remarking to Marcos: "We love your adherence to democratic principles and to democratic processes."[22] In September 1982, Marcos reached what was probably the high point in his relationship with Washington when he undertook a state visit to the United States.

Nevertheless, Marcos found himself under continued pressure from the constitutional opposition, the NPA, and the Moro National Liberation Front. American estimates were suggesting that the NPA now had some 7,500 armed regulars, while the MNLF was claiming to have 30,000 men under arms and to control 25 of the Philippines' southern provinces. The two guerrilla bodies had not, however, managed to form a common front--a development that Marcos was known to fear.

Moreover, the Philippine economy was in serious trouble. By 1980, the country had incurred $12.7 billion in foreign debt (a figure that had risen to $25 billion by 1983), and its trade balance was suffering from the sharp increases in oil prices in 1979. Twenty percent of export earnings were being used to pay debts, and the price of sugar, the Philippines' main export commodity, had fallen sharply.[23] The political impact of these problems was aggravated by the vivid contrast between, on the one hand, the lavish spending of the Marcos family and its associates and, on the other, the increasing misery of poorer Filipinos. While Imelda Marcos spent $31 million on a guesthouse entirely constructed of coconuts and $21 million on a film center, malnutrition spread in the shantytowns of Manila and in rural areas such as the sugar-growing island of Negros, where large numbers of workers were no longer paid after the fall in commodity prices and were unable to feed their families. In 1979, a World Bank study noted that in the Philippines "one-third to one-half of the population [was] too poor to purchase and consume enough food." In the face of such misery and continual abuse by local soldiers and police, some peasants began to work for the NPA and the MNLF, and the Catholic Church began openly to attack the Marcos regime.

Partly to assuage his nationalist critics, Marcos sought to hold the first review of the 1979 Military Bases Agreement in 1983, and the United States agreed. Despite the favored treatment he was receiving from the Reagan administration, Marcos played up (as he had with Carter) the possibility of improving relations with the Soviets should the Americans adopt a bargaining position he considered unacceptable. The Reagan administration, fully committed to improving its naval position in the western Pacific, proved more than willing to strike a deal with the Philippine president, and negotiations were completed within six weeks.

The 1983 Military Bases Agreement in fact produced few significant changes in the terms of the agreement. Its most outstanding feature was a pledge by the Americans to make their "best efforts" to secure from Congress $900 million in security assistance for the Philippines over a five-year period. Divided into three categories, the $900 million proposal exceeded the total amount of indirect compensation ($876 million) given by the United States to the Philippines for access to the bases between 1947 and 1977. For the Americans, the negotiations were seen as a success primarily because they had been able to secure access to their most valuable Pacific bases at a time when the current administration was rededicating itself to the preservation of naval supremacy in the region. For the Marcos regime, the $900 million "best effort" pledge by the United States seemed to provide the means for continued control of the islands well into the late 1980s.

However satisfactory the spring 1983 agreement was for the two governments, to many Filipinos it suggested that the Reagan administration was prepared to back an undemocratic government as long as the dictator in question continued to allow US bases on Philippine soil. Anti-American resentment grew accordingly. Then, on August 21 Aquino boarded a flight from Taiwan for the short flight to Manila.

THE REGIME UNDER ATTACK

By the spring of 1983, Aquino had decided to return to the Philippines to rally the opposition for the National Assembly elections scheduled for May 1984. He believed that Marcos might still be willing to accept a peaceful transfer of power.[24] Marcos opposed Aquino's return and sent several warnings to his political opponent, including one delivered in New York by Imelda Marcos herself. She told Aquino that there were elements in the Philippines that would try to assassinate him if he returned.

After the assassination, the Philippine government announced that a then-unidentified assassin had killed Aquino and that the military had killed the assassin. But few Filipinos believed that version of the assassination. It was generally assumed that Marcos had ordered the murder or that it had been carried out by the military in the belief that he would approve. Marcos's problems were compounded by the fact that he was sick, suffering from *lupus erythematosus*, a degenerative disease that appears in cycles and frequently attacks the kidneys, lungs, and heart. The Philippine public was generally aware that Marcos was ill, although they were not aware of the precise nature of his illness.[25] Shortly before the assassination Marcos had disappeared from public view, allegedly to write a book. In fact, he had secretly undergone his first kidney transplant.

In Manila, speculation grew that Imelda Marcos and Fabian Ver (by now chief of staff) had arranged the assassination while Marcos was incapacitated. Constitutionally, upon the president's death power would pass to a fifteen-member executive committee, which had been appointed by Marcos. Imelda Marcos was a member of the executive committee, and she clearly wished to succeed her husband. That prospect frightened many inside and outside the Philippines.

In any event, the assassination provoked an unprecedented demonstration of anti-Marcos sentiment. Aquino's body was moved to his birthplace in the northern province of Tarlac, where in two days more than 50,000 mourners paid their respects. Aquino was buried in Manila, and more than one million people lined the streets for his funeral there.

The day after the assassination, Marcos appeared on television, his first public appearance in three weeks, to condemn the assassination. He pointed out that Aquino had been warned about the danger of returning and suggested that only the Communists would benefit from the killing. The Philippine government continued to claim that the assassination was the work of a lone gunman acting on his own or possibly at the direction of the Communists; opposition leaders continued to charge publicly that Marcos and the army were responsible.[26]

In response to the protests, Marcos named a commission to investigate the assassination, but only his cronies agreed to join it. Two months later, after protests by Filipinos and from the international community, a second panel was named, this one led by Corazon Juliano-Agrava, a respected jurist.

But commissions of enquiry could not undo the political damage that the assassination had done to Marcos, mainly in turning the Philippine middle class--which had strongly supported him before and during the martial law period--against the president. In the weeks following the assassination, more and more anti-Marcos public demonstrations were held. As the protests continued, opposition leaders learned they could tweak the dictator and that he would (or could) not respond. The opposition thus became emboldened, and more open opposition to Marcos developed. On September 21, one month after the assassination (and also the eleventh anniversary of the imposition of martial law), a large demonstration in Manila erupted into violence, leaving eleven people dead.

By this point, some lower-level analysts in the United States had already suggested that Marcos's days as a head of state were numbered. In September 1982, the intelligence community had produced a special estimate warning that all was not well in the Philippines and citing growing opposition to Marcos. This view was shared by Philippines specialists such as Marjorie Niehaus, an analyst at the Congressional Research Service (who a year later was to become the Philippines analyst in the Department of State's Bureau of Intelligence and Research [INR]).

The problem was to identify a successor, individual or collective, who would be politically credible and likely to respect American interests. Contrary to many skeptical colleagues in Washington, Niehaus argued that there were in fact capable opposition leaders, including Corazon Aquino.

Although the US government was not ready to abandon Marcos, the assassination crystallized the private doubts of some officials about the Marcos regime. In particular, US ambassador Michael Armacost, who had until this point loyally implemented the Reagan policy of support for Marcos, underwent a conversion that he later described as "traumatic." In the events surrounding Aquino's death he saw "a government out of control."[27] Accordingly, Armacost made the politically courageous gesture of paying a condolence call on Aquino's widow, Corazon, and also attending the funeral mass.

Moreover, the size and fervor of the public demonstrations reportedly surprised US Embassy staff, prompting some observers to draw parallels with earlier events in Iran where, in order to propitiate the government, American officials had kept their contacts with the opposition to a minimum.[28] After the Aquino funeral, the embassy began to quietly establish closer communication with opposition leaders and with Cardinal Sin, by general consent the shrewdest and most influential of Marcos's critics.

Immediately after the assassination, the US Department of State released a statement condemning the murder as a "cowardly and despicable act." The statement used the term "political assassination"--a considered choice, since some of Marcos's henchmen were spreading the story that the murder was the settling of an old score by one of Aquino's personal enemies. The strength and speed of the statement itself reflected the efforts of John F. Maisto, another influential if relatively junior Washington opponent of Marcos. Maisto was desk officer for the Philippines at the State Department and had extensive contacts in the country, partly through his Filipina wife.

The assassination received heavy coverage in the *New York Times* and the *Washington Post*. On August 25, the *Times* carried a front-page article

quoting State Department officials as saying the United States would dissoci-
ate itself from Marcos if he were found to be implicated in the assassination.
Pressure built up for the cancellation of a visit to Manila by President Reagan
planned for the following November.

Reagan did eventually cancel the visit, as well as stops in Indonesia and
Thailand, to the consternation of those two countries.[29] But his continuing
trust in Marcos was expressed in a letter privately carried to Manila by
Michael Deaver, then Reagan's chief of staff. The letter began: "Dear Ferdinand and Imelda: I've always had confidence in your ability to handle things."
It closed: "Our friendship for you remains as warm and firm as does our
feeling for the people of the Philippines."[30] (Reagan, a State Department
official once said in exasperation, saw Marcos as if he were "a hero on a
bubble gum card he had collected as a kid."[31])

More publicly, Vice-President Bush rejected any suggestion of distancing
from Marcos, declaring on October 10 that the United States could "not cut
away from a person who, imperfect though he may be on human rights, has
worked with us."[32] In a further interview, the Vice-President added, rather
enigmatically: "The United States does not want to have another Khomeini."[33]

Similar thinking by analogy appeared during the presidential election
debates in 1984. At one point President Reagan was asked how, given his
criticisms of President Carter over the handling of the fall of the shah and
Somoza, he proposed to deal with any similar crisis concerning Marcos.
"What," his questioner asked, "should you do and what can you do to prevent
the Philippines from becoming another Nicaragua?" Reagan responded: "I
know there are things there in the Philippines that do not look good to us
from the standpoint right now of democratic rights, but what is the alternative? . . . It is a large Communist movement."[34] This remark provoked
complaints that Reagan was ignoring or unfairly dismissing the constitutional
opposition in the Philippines. Finally, in February 1985, Reagan acknowledged
that there was an opposition that was "pledged to democracy." But this admis-
sion, grudging as it was, did not significantly undermine the president's attach-
ment to Marcos.

As demonstrations continued, Marcos himself threatened the reimposi-
tion of martial law, and the Catholic Church, a focal point of the opposition,
urged calm. From this point, Marcos seemed to withdraw politically into a
narrow circle of advisers, the most important of whom were his wife, Eduardo
"Danding" Cojuangco (a cousin of Corazon Aquino) who had sided with
Marcos and eventually fled the country with him, and Fabian Ver. Politically,
he turned more and more toward the military, and particularly toward Ver, for
support.

But to many of the younger officers, Ver symbolized what was wrong with the Philippine military. After imposing martial law, Marcos had expanded the military from 58,000 to over 200,000 and placed the Philippine constabulary under the control of the armed forces. He increased the military budget, but much of the money went into the pockets of senior officers, many of whom acquired lucrative business contracts and some of whom were believed to be selling arms to insurgents. Marcos's dependence on Ver created discontent among the officer corps of the Philippine armed forces, leading to the formation of a secret group called the Reform the Armed Forces Now Movement (RAM) headed by Lt. Gen. Fidel Ramos, a West Point graduate, head of the constabulary and Integrated National Police, and a respected (if tough) professional soldier.

The US Congress and the Philippines

The Aquino assassination sharpened congressional interest in the Philippines. Congressman Stephen Solarz, a Democrat from New York and chairman of the House Subcommittee on Asian and Pacific Affairs, traveled to the Philippines and paid a condolence call on the Aquino family. Following the assassination, Solarz became increasingly critical of the Marcos government, drawing attention to its growing unpopularity and calling frequently for decreased military assistance to the Philippines and increased economic aid. Solarz's efforts clearly provided encouragement to the Philippine opposition and probably served to hold down anti-American sentiment in the administration that came to power after Marcos was ousted.

In the spring of 1984, the US Senate Foreign Relations Committee, chaired by Senator Charles Percy (R-IL), began to take a critical look at the Philippines. In May, June, and July, two Foreign Relations Committee staffers, Frederick Z. Brown and Carl Ford, traveled extensively in the Philippines on a fact-finding mission. (The following February, Ford was to become the CIA's national intelligence officer for East Asia and the Pacific.) Brown and Ford reported finding "a disciplined, purposeful communist insurgency" which was becoming "a major threat to the Philippine democracy." They also commented on the state of the regime in Manila: "There has been a profound loss of confidence in President Marcos and his ability to govern. The country's leadership is virtually bankrupt in terms of public confidence. There appears to be little popular expectation that the leadership will act for the good of the country as opposed to its own narrow interests."[35] The Brown and Ford report focused the attention of the Foreign Relations Committee onto the Philippines. Richard Lugar (R-IN), who became chairman in January 1985, was to play a crucial role in the formation of US policy in the final days of the crisis and in building bipartisan policy support on Capitol Hill.[36]

Early in 1985, the Solarz subcommittee recommended that military sales credits for that year be decreased from $50 million to $25 million and that economic aid be increased from the $95 million requested by the administration to $155 million. The subcommittee intended the changes to facilitate political, economic, and military reform and to demonstrate to the Filipinos that the aid was "not for the benefit of any particular leader or faction."[37] The Senate Foreign Relations Committee added an amendment to the foreign aid bill saying that Congress would determine future aid to the Philippines according to enhancement of US security interests and sufficient progress by the Philippine government in, among other things, guaranteeing free and fair elections and ensuring the prosecution of Aquino's assassin.

The Policy Network

Meanwhile, a significant network of generally like-minded officials had formed around the question of policy toward the Philippines. In January 1984, Stephen W. Bosworth replaced Armacost as ambassador in Manila. Bosworth, though not especially liberal in philosophy, began his tenure with a clear skepticism toward Marcos and, unlike many of his predecessors, he was never seduced by the high-living ambience at the presidential palace. On the contrary, he quickly established easy and confidential relations with Cardinal Sin and other opposition leaders. Consequently, Bosworth became a valuable and independent source of guidance for his colleagues in Washington, as well as an important point of communication with the opposition as the crisis worsened.

Bosworth's predecessor, Armacost, far from losing influence with his transfer home, became undersecretary of state for political affairs, and was thus in a good position to express his disenchantment with Marcos. Indeed, it was the Department of State that emerged as leader in the making of policy toward the Philippines, the main official involved being Paul Wolfowitz, assistant secretary of state for East Asian and Pacific affairs. Wolfowitz worked closely with Assistant Secretary of Defense for International Security Affairs Richard Armitage and with NSC Asian specialists Gaston Sigur and Richard Childress. Armitage later noted that there was "an unbelievable unanimity of views at the assistant secretary level"--a unanimity he attributed to the fact that all concerned (with the exception of Childress, a military officer) were political appointees: "We all had the same views about supporting the president. The president was our highest priority. By background, we were all Asian special- ists. That was our background by proclivity, by education, by experience, so you had people who were doing the policy-making who had experience, who knew the players personally, who had no bureaucratic conflicts. We were all there to support the president. We met regularly."[38]

Throughout the period of this case, US policymakers were well served by official reporting from Manila and by the intelligence analysis produced in Washington, both at CIA and in INR at State. Reporting from the US Embassy in Manila was excellent. In addition to producing accurate and timely intelligence analyses, key CIA officers in Washington had good contact with policymakers at the assistant secretary level. The director of CIA's Office of East Asia and the national intelligence officer for East Asia, Carl Ford, both had good working relationships with Wolfowitz, Armitage, and the NSC staff. The CIA was thus able to bring its intelligence judgments directly to policymakers at the assistant secretary level.

The secretaries of state and defense read little intelligence on the Philip- pines, relying primarily on oral briefings. Secretary of State George Shultz listened to Armacost; Secretary of Defense Weinberger listened (though not uncritically) to Armitage and Admiral Crowe, at this time commander in chief of US forces in the Pacific and shortly to become chairman of the joint chiefs of staff.

Crowe had reached the conclusion that "things had to change" in the Philippines and had taken the unusual step (for a serving officer) of giving political advice to both Marcos and Reagan.[39] He found Shultz willing to listen, but still undecided. He got nowhere on this subject with either Wein- berger or Director of Central Intelligence William J. Casey. Nevertheless, Crowe's advocacy meant (in Bonner's words) "that State did not have to fight the Pentagon as it so often did over Philippine policy and in many other parts of the world."[40]

EXERCISES

After reading this case up to this point, write a short memorandum identify- ing and discussing the main differences in the way that the Philippine problem was handled by and within the US government, compared with the Nicaraguan and Iranian cases.

Arguments About the Succession

In the fall of 1984 and the winter of 1985, Washington conducted a formal review of US policy toward the Philippines. The NSC staff issued the terms of reference, but State drafted the new policy paper (initially written by John Maisto). The review resulted in the adoption in January 1985 of a policy directive signed by President Reagan.

The directive saw Marcos as part of the problem, but as also necessarily part of the solution: "We need to be able to work with [Marcos] and to try to influence him through a well-orchestrated policy of incentives and disincentives to set the stage for a peaceful and eventual transition to a successor government whenever that takes place."[41] The United States, the directive declared, did not "want to remove Marcos from power or destabilize [his government]."[42] Rather, the aim was to induce reform by both pressure and incentives--to work to revitalize democratic institutions, to dismantle crony capitalism, and to restore professional, apolitical leadership to the Philippine military.

Although policymakers generally agreed on assessments of the Philippines, there was disagreement about the future course of US policy. Some State Department officers believed the new policy did not go far enough, that Marcos was the problem and could not be included in the solution. Morton Abramowitz, who became assistant secretary for intelligence and research at the State Department in early 1985, argued that there would be no improvement in the Philippines until Marcos left the scene. Some officers in State's Bureau of East Asian Affairs and some intelligence officers in State and CIA agreed, although the intelligence officers could not recommend policy in their analysis. Moreover, officials such as Abramowitz, Marjorie Niehaus, and John Maisto were too junior to be able to exercise direct influence on policy.

But there was still the problem of identifying an acceptable and authoritative successor. Those arguing that Marcos should leave the scene, including Abramowitz, realized that for the United States to withdraw support from Marcos with no identifiable alternative would be risky. US stakes in the Philippines were high: Marcos might be succeeded by someone less favorably disposed to the American bases. Moreover, all those involved in forming the new policy, and particularly the NSC staff, knew the president did not wish to withdraw support from Marcos.

Armitage explained later that the purpose of the new policy had been "to put pressure on Marcos":

He could either make the reforms or he would fall. We felt it was not a good thing to immediately put him in a corner. The reason was the opposition had not congealed. The Armed Forces of the Philippines (AFP) had not made their decision. We were, of course, aware from intelligence of the grumblings in the army and the splits and the divisions in the army. We thought it would be a horrible thing for the army to turn on itself, one faction against another. We felt it would be wrong to bring things to a head before there was a congealed opposition. So we gave Marcos a choice: he could either reform or he would have to go, realizing that reform was next to impossible for him. We constantly upped the ante on Marcos. First, it was getting rid of human rights abuses, then we wanted the over-staying generals out. And it worked.[43]

Cooperation between administration officials and Congress was crucial to pursuing this strategy, which involved allowing "the fruit to become rotten and drop from the tree without harming any of the other fruit."[44] In particular, consultation between Wolfowitz, Armitage, and Solarz enabled military assistance to the Philippine armed forces to continue, with the political benefit that the military did not become anti-American even as they began to consider action against Marcos.

One problem concerned the relative urgency with which different elements in the US government wanted to move. The Department of State were more intent on speedy action than those closer to the president, who felt that Reagan's influence over Marcos was an asset that should be guarded for use in a crisis that all sensed would eventually come.[45]

In line with the new policy, Wolfowitz, Armitage, and Childress visited the Philippines in January 1985, urging reform. They were followed by Armacost, Admiral Crowe, and CIA Director Casey. Casey, at least, came away convinced that Marcos had things well under control.

Marcos Counterattacks

In October 1984, while the US review of Philippine policy was still under-way, the Agrava Board released its findings on the assassination of Benigno Aquino. The majority report (four of five members) said a high-level military conspiracy was responsible for the murder. Ver, two other generals, six lower-ranking officers, sixteen enlisted men, and one civilian were cited as "indictable for the premeditated killing of Aquino."[46] Immediately after the report was issued, Marcos named a special prosecutor to bring charges. Ver was placed on leave of absence, and General Fidel Ramos was appointed chief of staff. The following January the special prosecutor filed charges against those blamed in the majority report.

The United States left little doubt about who it felt was responsible for the assassination. Immediately after the Agrava findings were released, the Department of State issued a statement urging Marcos to act on the majority report. A few days later, Ambassador Bosworth, in a speech to the Manila Rotary Club, warned against the concentration of political and economic power. Bosworth referred to Iran, where a concentration of power had, he said, brought the shah to a bad end.

In the spring and summer of 1985, opposition to Marcos and speculation on the succession were voiced more and more openly in the press. *Veritas*, a Catholic newspaper, and a radio station of the same name were strong voices for the opposition. In June 1985 the *San Jose Mercury News* ran a series of reports on secret investments in the United States by the Marcoses and several of their associates. The story was picked up by the Manila newspapers and soon became common knowledge in the Philippines.

Faced with an attempt to impeach him, Marcos developed a strategy to undermine the opposition. At a KBL caucus in early August, he raised the possibility of calling a snap presidential election rather than waiting for the scheduled one in 1987. His intent was clearly to catch the opposition when it was off guard and unable to unite on a candidate. Marcos clearly intended to win such an election, whatever that took, and he believed an election victory would restore his political credibility in Washington.

As the summer wore on, it became clear that Ver and the others being tried for the murder of Aquino would be acquitted. There was little doubt after the three-judge panel trying the alleged assassins threw out the testimony gathered by the Agrava Board because it violated the rights of the accused. As with the assassination, the Filipinos generally believed Marcos was behind the court decision.

Marcos certainly did not respond to US encouragement to effect reform.[47] In the spring of 1985 he charged publicly that the American media and certain elements in the US government were out to get him. Senate Foreign Relations Committee staffer Frederick Brown visited the Philippines again in August and, after a lengthy conversation with Marcos, wrote a report which included (among others) the following judgments:

1. President Marcos's prime objective is to stay in power, not to promote change which could endanger him in the short term. .... He does not accept his own mortality and expects to remain in power indefinitely. He hopes to manage the present crisis tactically, without yielding to terms from either the US or his countrymen.
2. Marcos has not gotten our message about the urgent need for reform. US demands for reform run diametrically counter to Marcos's interests.
3. Marcos believes that he enjoys the support of the highest levels of the US government. Congress may huff and puff, assistant secretaries may harass him, and some of his military aid monies may be transferred to ESF [economic support funds]. But in the end, he believes, the US will not pull its support. Many Filipinos seem to share this view.
4. Marcos is convinced that Clark and Subic give him the whip handle in dealing with the US.[48]

Solarz and others in Congress tried to keep up the pressure on Marcos. Solarz held hearings in October and November on the crisis in the Philippines, providing a platform for administration officials to emphasize the need for change.

Some in the United States were beginning to consider other ways of getting rid of Marcos. In August 1985, a conference on the Philippines was held at the National War College in Washington, at which the possibility of a covert operation to remove Marcos was discussed. It turned out that such a plan had already been mooted within the Department of Defense (and, according to some sources, the DOD and the CIA were already engaged in encouraging RAM (Ramos's secret organization within the Philippine armed forces). Some participants referred to the precedent of the assassination of President Ngo Dinh Diem of Vietnam in 1963 "and what had happened after the Kennedy administration had, actively or passively, endorsed the coup in which he was murdered."[49]

Marcos was well aware of differences of opinion among American policymakers and clearly would not respond to any pressure unless it came directly from President Reagan or someone close to him. In August, he laid out of his view of Washington to a PBS interviewer:

Your government is divided into bureaucratic factions. There is one faction there which closes its eyes to reality and has come out openly against my administration. There is another faction trying to help us. I won't mention names, but we have had some problems with former ambassadors who did not see eye-to-eye with some of our people here. . . . I am told that these are the leaders in the anti-Marcos movement within that faction. The story in the diplomatic circles is that in Washington you need two ambassadors--one for Congress and another for the Executive Department.[50]

In these circumstances, the president was prevailed on to send Senator Laxalt, a Republican from Nevada and a friend and confidant, to see Marcos. Only a personal emissary from the president could, it was felt, break Marcos's conviction that he was simply the object of a State Department plot. He was to confirm that the US president was himself concerned.[51] Specifically, Laxalt was to communicate Reagan's concern "about the general political instability in the Philippines" and to determine whether Marcos still enjoyed the support of the people.[52]

In October, Laxalt visited Manila, and he and Marcos discussed Reagan's concerns at length. Laxalt pointed out that congressional pressure was causing a problem. Marcos listened but, according to Bosworth who also was present at the meeting, showed no sign that he was about to reform. Laxalt sensed that Marcos was out of touch with his own people: His isolation had altered his perception of his country's problems and of his own popularity. Laxalt reported that he suggested Marcos go ahead with the idea of a snap election, an idea that he claimed had earlier been raised with Marcos by William Casey.[53] Laxalt found that Marcos was apparently uninterested in a snap election.

Critics (including some in the embassy in Manila) were disappointed by the Laxalt visit, one describing it as "a love feast."[54] In their view, Laxalt was too easily impressed by Marcos and failed to push him on the need for reforms. Indeed, Laxalt went as far as to suggest to Marcos that he hire a public relations firm to mend his image in the United States.[55] From Marcos's point of view, Laxalt was a valuable new friend--one who could give him better access to Reagan and make him less dependent on less friendly, lower-level officials (notably Bosworth).

Indeed, Marcos did call Laxalt frequently by phone after their October meetings. His use of this channel reflected his increasing conviction that US diplomats in Manila (and probably the State Department and the CIA, too) were planning to murder him a la Diem.[56] In the course of one talk, Laxalt raised the idea of a snap election. Laxalt suggested the announcement of an early election be made on the television program, *This Week with David Brinkley,* in order to capture American attention. On November 3, Marcos took Laxalt's suggestion and announced that he was calling a snap election. The announcement was big news in the United States, but being made on a Sunday morning in the United States meant it was made in the middle of the night Philippines time--one more indication that Marcos was out of touch with or contemptuous of his own people.

As he later admitted, the decision itself showed how much out of touch he was. It was, he told Stanley Karnow in 1987, the "biggest mistake" of his life.[57] Indeed, his immediate advisers unanimously advised him against an election (he actually made the decision when Imelda was away on a trip to Moscow). Yet the political attractions of an election were obvious. If he won (especially if he won without too much fraud--or without too much being observed), he would have confounded American and domestic critics who claimed that he was simply a dictator. He would have secured a new six-year term, during which he could arrange a transfer of power to one of his family or to a political associate like Ver.

The state of the opposition must have added to the temptation to call an election. His opponents were badly divided, and Marcos could reasonably assume that they would be unable to agree on a candidate--least of all on a soft-mannered "housewife" such as Corazon Aquino. Aquino had had no experience in office and had not actively sought to be a candidate. And, in fact, the opposition did not agree to unify behind her until the eleventh hour.

Marcos's premises, if not his aims, were shared by State Department officials, who reacted with private dismay to the news. They believed that the opposition was not yet ready to beat Marcos and feared that a stolen victory by Marcos would only benefit the guerrillas (as well as giving him another six years to ruin the Philippines).[58] Their strategy assumed the use of the 1986 municipal elections to prepare the opposition for the 1987 presidential election.

The White House and Marcos's sympathizers were, however, pleased by the election decision. Laxalt assured members of the Senate that the election would be clean, since (he reasoned) it would do Marcos no good to win an election colored by cheating.[59]

The February 1986 Election

Marcos set the election date for February 7. On December 1, the same day Marcos announced the election date, Ver and the twenty-five other defendants in the Aquino murder trial were acquitted. Ver was reinstated as chief of staff.

This decision made the military plotters in RAM all the more determined to stage a coup. Led by two colonels in Defense Minister Enrile's security unit, they had begun some serious (though also very indiscrete) planning for a coup.[60] Their original plan was to move after the scheduled presidential election in May 1987, assuming that Marcos would rig the election and that they could capitalize on the public reaction.

The US government, through the defense attache at the Manila embassy, discouraged an early coup without discouraging the notion of some eventual military action. The intelligence community judgment was that, although members of RAM were discontented with Marcos, most senior officers in the Philippine military would support the president if RAM attempted a coup.

After Marcos announced the snap election, the group decided to move on February 23. It planned to storm the presidential palace, remove Marcos from power, and install a civilian-military leadership that would include Enrile, Ramos, and Corazon Aquino.[61] The plotters reportedly also planned to invite Cardinal Sin and some other respected Philippine military and political figures to join the new government. The coup plot, while never actually carried out, was to force events in the final days of the crisis.

In December, the Solarz subcommittee began an investigation into the Marcoses' property holdings in the United States. Testimony at the hearing received wide press coverage in the United States and in the Philippines, where the election campaign was underway. The hearings continued up through Marcos's ouster and focused attention on the Marcoses' extensive holdings in the US.

On December 2, Corazon Aquino announced her candidacy, and on December 11, Aquino and Salvador "Doy" Laurel, leader of the opposition coalition UNIDO, agreed to run for president and vice-president, respectively, as the opposition's slate against Marcos.[62] Cardinal Sin was crucial in persuading Aquino to accept Laurel as her vice-presidential running mate and in getting Laurel to take second place on the ticket. He reportedly told Laurel quite bluntly: "Cory is more popular than you are. Make the sacrifice, or Marcos will win."[63] In persuading the two candidates, it helped that the cardinal could tell each that "the American embassy was of the same mind."[64]

Aquino's campaign, which (like Marcos's) was heavily directed toward American public opinion, got off to a difficult start as the result of an interview she gave in December to A. M. Rosenthal, executive editor of the *New York Times*. Unused to such interviews, Aquino acknowledged her inexperience and offered a number of half-considered thoughts, suggesting notably that she would like to see the US bases removed at some time and that she would, if elected, declare a ceasefire and open a "dialogue" with the NPA. Rosenthal, a hard-line Cold Warrior, returned to the United States appalled by what he saw as her naivety. President Reagan was much impressed by Rosenthal's report and quoted it frequently against those who wanted to dump Marcos. This initial disaster did, however, spur American friends of Aquino into organizing a "support group" that arranged for the hiring of a New York public relations firm to work on her behalf and provided money and people to help the campaign. The "Friends of Aquino" enjoyed the surreptitious support of the American Embassy and Secretary of State Shultz.[65]

Although the opposition had agreed on one presidential candidate, Marcos was still confident of victory and determined to win it, by whatever means. He and his vice-presidential candidate, Senator Arturo ("Jukebox") Tolentino, ran very hard against the Communist threat to the Philippines, stressing that Aquino was not capable of dealing with the NPA insurgency.[66] In campaigning, Marcos frequently recalled his experiences in World War II, claiming to have been a guerrilla fighter against the Japanese and to have been wounded five times. Just two weeks before the election, however, Marcos's war record was called into question by an American historian who had discovered in official files that the US military never accepted Marcos's claims. Marcos was stung by this revelation, which was given heavy coverage by the Philippine media, and by the *New York Times* and the *Washington Post*.

During the campaign Marcos's health again became an issue (by now, he had lost his second kidney), and his public appearances were carefully rationed. Aquino's campaign appearances, on the other hand, were frequent and she drew huge crowds. Aquino pulled no punches, countering Marcos's frequent charge that she had no experience by stressing that, indeed, she could not match the president's experience "in cheating, stealing, lying or assassinating political opponents." Aquino also began to gain with her American audience as, under the tutelage of her advisers, she modified her earlier positions. The US bases, she now said, "would not be a major campaign issue."

Most public polls, nevertheless, predicted a Marcos victory. Filipinos, it was said, would pray for Aquino but vote for Marcos. In December, the intelligence community judgment was that Marcos would win an honest election by a narrow margin. By January, the election was too close to call, and on the eve of the vote the intelligence community predicted an actual Aquino victory but that Marcos would rig the results to win.

On January 30, President Reagan announced that a bipartisan US observer delegation (led by Senator Lugar and Congressman John Murtha, D-PA) would visit the Philippines during the election. Reagan's statement tied the conduct of the election and the subsequent pursuit of reform to American aid. If the election was fair and was followed by genuine economic, political, and military reform, he promised: "We should consider, in consultation with the Congress, a significantly larger program of economic and military assistance for the Philippines for the next five years."[67]

Reagan and his immediate advisers remained deeply skeptical of Aquino. Shortly before the election, Chief of Staff Donald Regan declared that even if Marcos were elected by "massive fraud," the United States would still "have to do business with Marcos. There are a lot of governments," [Regan added] "elected by fraud."[68] Conservative columnists such as Jeane Kirkpatrick similarly criticized liberals for singling out Marcos: There were, she estimated, at least one hundred states in the UN "probably governed more poorly than the Philippines." Kirkpatrick went on to invoke the familiar list of authoritarian friends of America whose demise liberals had blithely arranged, only to find something much nastier coming out of the woodwork: "Remember [she asked] Fulgencio Batista of Cuba, Ngo Dinh Diem of Vietnam, Lon Nol of Cambodia, the shah of Iran, Anastasio Somoza of Nicaragua ?"[69]

The US observer delegation went to the Philippines and fanned out throughout the country to witness voting at various polling stations. Many observers witnessed fraud by the ruling party. Voters were disenfranchised and, although the vote count may have been accurately recorded at polling places, the totals made public in Manila suggested the figures were being changed to insure a Marcos victory. The official vote count was slow, which suggested to Lugar that something was amiss. Competing figures were put out by two organizations. The National Citizens Movement for Free Elections (NAMFREL), a citizens' group intent on detecting and exposing fraud by the regime, published vote totals showing Aquino ahead.[70] COMELEC, the official vote-counting body, showed Marcos winning.

The day after the election, members of the observer group met in Manila to discuss their findings.[71] That evening some thirty workers at COMELEC left their posts and sought refuge in a nearby church, charging that the government was rigging the results to ensure a victory for Marcos. Members of the US observer team visited the COMELEC defectors and found very convincing evidence of fraud by the ruling party.

On February 10, President Reagan declared that he was reserving judgment on the charges of fraud in the election. He expressed the hope that Marcos and Aquino "could come together to make sure the government works."

The following day, Lugar returned to Washington and (accompanied by Bosworth) reported to Reagan. The president seemed not to be listening, and at one point he claimed to have seen on television pictures of Aquino supporters throwing ballots out onto a street. Lugar was baffled by this remark. Though it later turned out that the ballot-dumpers were in fact Marcos's men, this scene had imprinted itself on Reagan's memory, with disastrous consequences.

Next day, the White House released a guarded statement declaring that it was still too earlier for an official judgement but acknowledging that the election had been "flawed by reports of fraud, which we take seriously, and by violence." The statement continued: "This concerns us because we cherish commitment to free and fair elections and because we believe the government of the Philippines needs an authentic popular mandate in order effectively to counter a growing communist insurgency and restore health to its troubled economy."[72]

At this point there was strong evidence that fraud had occurred, but the White House was said to fear that condemning Marcos outright might cause him to declare the elections null and void. Moreover, there was still strong resistance within the president's inner circle to discarding Marcos. Despite the evidence, Reagan (in Stanley Karnow's words) "preferred his own eccentric sources"--not least Imelda Marcos, who was perpetually on the phone to Nancy Reagan.[73] Chief of Staff Donald Regan (who had very little knowledge of the Philippines) and Director of Central Intelligence William Casey were pressing Reagan to stand by Marcos.

NEGOTIATING THE SUCCESSION

On February 11, Reagan agreed to the sending of Ambassador Philip Habib to the Philippines to assess the situation. Habib was a diplomatic veteran whom Reagan had used before on sensitive fact-finding missions. He was to meet with Marcos and Aquino and with other Philippine leaders and report his findings to the president. Upon hearing that Habib was to visit the Philippines, Aquino feared that he might be going to urge her to join with Marcos in a coalition government.[74] As soon as Habib met Aquino, he assured her that such was not his mission and that he was there to assess the situation.[75] He spent over a week in the Philippines and met with several Filipino leaders, including Marcos, Aquino, Cardinal Sin, and key cabinet ministers. Some of the cabinet ministers told Habib that Marcos was finished. In particular, Habib was impressed by defense minister Enrile, who gave the impression that he was separating himself from Marcos and might soon "reveal his hand."[76] Habib decided that it was time to tell Reagan that Marcos had run his course.

However, on the evening of February 11--the very day that he had announced Habib's appointment--Reagan held a news conference which nearly destroyed the carefully developed relationship between the American Embassy in Manila and Aquino. In response to a follow-up question about the effect of a tainted election in the Philippines, the president said: "Well, I think that we're concerned about the violence that was evident there and the possibility of fraud, although it could have been that all of that was occurring on both sides. But at the same time, we're encouraged by the fact that it's evident that there is a two-party system in the Philippines and a pluralism that I think would benefit their people."[77]

This statement pleased Marcos (the videotape was played over and over on Manila television) and infuriated Aquino: "I would wonder," she said, "at the motives of a friend of democracy who chose to conspire with Mr. Marcos to cheat the Filipino people of their liberation." Bosworth went to Aquino and assured her that the US position was evolving.[78] The ambassador urged her to be patient, hinting that she would be pleased with the eventual US position.

Bosworth also had to calm down his own staff, several of whom were upset by the president's statement. He complained vigorously to Shultz about Reagan's statement; the secretary of state replied, "Okay, you've made your point. Now relax. We'll try to fix it."

At home, other officials and politicians distanced themselves from Reagan. Breaking Republican ranks, Lugar felt bound to say publicly that the president was "not well informed." On February 13, Senators Sam Nunn (D-GA), the ranking Democrat on the Armed Services Committee, and Bob Dole (R-KS), Republican majority leader, both said the United States should cut off aid to the Philippines if Marcos was elected through fraud.

In the aftermath, the intelligence community provided convincing evidence to the NSC staff and the president that the ruling party had engaged in fraud on a massive scale. On February 14, the Catholic bishops of the Philippines issued a statement condemning fraud in the election and urging nonviolent resistance. Two days later, the pope supported the bishops' statement.

Finally, on February 15, a major US policy shift became evident when the Western White House issued a statement acknowledging that the elections had been "marred by widespread fraud and violence perpetrated largely by the ruling party."[79] The "fraud on both sides" line had been dropped. Moreover, unnamed White House officials told the press that Marcos should start planning for the succession.

Two days later Lugar called on Marcos to resign. Lugar's role in shaping US policy on the Philippines was extremely important. A moderate-conservative Republican, Lugar was generally regarded as unprejudiced on the Philippines, and he clearly had an impact on thinking at the White House. On February 19, the Senate passed a resolution by 85 to 9 condemning the election as fraudulent. The following day, the House Foreign Affairs Committee voted unanimously to stop all military aid to the Philippines. Wolfowitz and Armitage had privately urged Solarz not to end all military aid, arguing that such a step might cause Philippine military morale to collapse. Speaking at a Council on Foreign Relations meeting, Wolfowitz urged his colleagues not to be too hasty in disowning Marcos, lest chaos follow: reportedly, he was concerned about "another Iran, another Nicaragua" and the consequences for Republican party fortunes. In Congress, Solarz responded that Marcos was the best thing the Communists had going in the Philippines.

Thus, by February 22 it was clear that Marcos had perpetrated massive fraud in the election and that Aquino was not about to give in. The White House had accepted that Marcos had cheated to win the election. Nevertheless, a major policy problem remained. COMELEC said Marcos had won the election, while NAMFREL maintained that Aquino was the victor. Aquino had announced a policy of nonviolent resistance to bring Marcos down, and she seemed to have much support among Filipinos.

For his part, Marcos had several options. He could simply claim the presidency and wait Aquino out. He could declare the election null and void. And he could still legally declare martial law and rule by decree. Neither the US policymakers nor the intelligence analysts saw a quick and easy resolution of the crisis that would leave Marcos out. Nor, presumably, did Reagan, who had not yet been convinced that Marcos should go.

Military Revolt and "People Power"

The coup plot broke the stalemate, but only just, and it almost served Marcos's purposes. The coup was still scheduled for February 23, but by February 20, Marcos had learned of the plot.[80] He arrested some of the lower ranking officers involved, and their interrogation implicated Enrile. On February 22, Enrile learned that Marcos was aware of the coup and, fearing arrest, convinced Ramos to join him at Camp Aguinaldo in Manila, where both would announce that they had broken from Marcos.

Enrile and Ramos went to Camp Aguinaldo and called a press conference. Enrile announced that "Marcos did not really win this election." Enrile then described how he had personally stolen votes for Marcos. Neither Enrile nor Ramos mentioned the coup plot. Marcos did, and actually had one of the junior officers testify on television, but by that time no one any longer believed the Philippine president. Most Filipinos believed the coup report was just another Marcos trick.

Aquino was at this time in Cebu City, some 400 miles south of Manila. At Enrile's request, Aquino phoned supporters in Manila and asked them to go to Camp Aguinaldo. While Aquino was in Cebu City, the United States offered her sanctuary on a US Navy ship. She declined the offer.

After Enrile and Ramos announced their break with Marcos, the US Embassy urged press correspondents to go to Camp Aguinaldo, where televised reports of Enrile and Ramos were soon beamed around the world.[81] In addition to providing good television footage, the rebellion became a rallying point for Aquino supporters. This was where "people power" developed. Cardinal Sin, after learning that Enrile and Ramos had defected, urged Aquino supporters to go to Camp Aguinaldo and show their support for the anti-Marcos movement.

The people went. At one point there were between one and two million Filipinos surrounding Camp Aguinaldo. Television coverage was continuous, and satellite transmission brought it to America live. Ramos and Enrile moved from Camp Aguinaldo to Camp Crame, across the street, because it was easier to defend. When Enrile walked from Camp Aguinaldo to Camp Crame, he was engulfed in a sea of supporters and, upon arriving at Camp Crame, looked out at some one million people cheering and chanting for Corazon Aquino.

By February 23 it had become clear that military suppression of Enrile and Ramos would involve many civilian casualties. Marcos had the force available. In fact, Ver is reported to have ordered a marine general to attack the rebel headquarters at Camp Crame: At one point a column of marine tanks, armored personnel carriers, and trucks of armed marines drove toward Camp Crame, but the column stopped just short of the people surrounding the camp and the marines were presented with flowers by young women at the front of the crowd. Much of this was beamed around the world on color television.

Less apparent was some discreet American support for the revolution. CIA technicians occupied a backroom at the Defense Ministry in Camp Aguinaldo, putting out false reports about defections by Marcos troops in order to lower morale among the president's supporters. The CIA also provided a new transmitter for Radio *Veritas* when Marcos's troops broke into and destroyed its own transmitter, which was a major means of communication for the opposition. Rebel helicopters were refueled and rearmed by American personnel at Clark Air Base, and American communications specialists intercepted all Ver's orders to his troops, passing them on to Enrile and Ramos.

Within hours after the statements by Enrile and Ramos, the White House commented on the new developments, arguing that they confirmed its view that the elections now lacked credibility. But the statement (which originated in the State Department) stopped short of suggesting that Marcos resign.

DISCUSSION QUESTIONS

1. *What in your view should have been the main considerations determining US policy at this point?*
2. *What were the main options available to US policymakers? What were the merits as well as the risks and uncertainties associated with each?*
3. *What leverage did the United States have to bring about a "successful" outcome?*
4. *To what extent had the United States brought about the situation in which "people power" became effective?*
5. *Should the United States have tried to begin negotiations with Marcos and/or the opposition at this point?*
6. *What might the agenda for such negotiations have been? Who might have been invited?*

NEGOTIATING THE SUCCESSION:
ENDGAME

On Saturday, February 22, Shultz conferred with his assistant Charles Hill, Armacost, and Wolfowitz. Shultz suggested that since Marcos was clearly "unraveling," the time had come for the US government to tell the Philippine president to give up power, encouraging him with an offer of asylum. Armacost was concerned about the lack of a clear succession: The various factions were maneuvering among themselves, and it wasn't clear that the decisive moment had arrived. Shultz responded: "Once they see a major swing, they'll try to save themselves." Hill wanted a speedy decision, for if Marcos attacked, there would be a bloodbath: "We could see Enrile begging for his life and house arrest, and we'll end up with the Marcos dictatorship versus the Communists."[82]

The problem was, Shultz said, to get both principals to decide. Marcos would be stubborn, and Reagan was not "the guy to pull the plug on Marcos"-- especially if Marcos were to put the plug right back in. Then Reagan would be embarrassed and would be seen to have failed. The important thing, the group concluded, was to stop Marcos from using force: Bosworth was instructed to use all his influence to prevent this from happening. Meanwhile, a statement offering Marcos refuge in the United States would be prepared for presentation to Reagan.

That night, Habib returned to Washington and came to a meeting at Shultz's house early in the morning of the 23rd, a Sunday. Even before the meeting began, Shultz had received news from Bosworth that confirmed his fears: "Marcos will not draw the conclusion that he must leave unless President Reagan puts it to him directly. Go for a dignified transition out."[83] Even more ominously, Bosworth warned that Marcos might launch an attack at daybreak on Monday. It was already eight o'clock on Sunday evening in Manila.

The meeting was attended by Shultz, Weinberger, Crowe, National Security Assistant John Poindexter, and the CIA's deputy director for intelligence, Robert Gates; also present were Armacost, Wolfowitz, Habib, and Armitage.[84] Habib took the lead, announcing his verdict that Marcos had "had it." The Philippine president, he said, refused to recognize that he faced "a widespread movement to dump him."

If Marcos didn't surrender power there would, Habib thought, be a sharp polarization that would benefit the Communists. It would be another of those "total shifts," such as had occurred when Diem was killed and when the shah fell. They were always costly for the United States: "We pay a heavy price for our past." On the other hand--Habib continued--if Marcos could be edged out, Aquino would be a stronger leader than they might suspect and she had already given him assurances that she would respect the base agreements.

Weinberger was still worried about what would happen after Marcos left. Habib responded that this would not be "another Iran." There was an organized and democratically led opposition backed by the full authority of the Catholic Church, and there wasn't the anti-Americanism found in Iran. Like Hill the day before, Habib pressed for a speedy and firm decision: The longer the situation was left to deteriorate, the less influence the US government would be able to exercise over it.

As in the smaller Saturday meeting, the group concluded that Marcos was beyond political salvation. But at least one heated exchange took place over what to do next. Habib immediately scotched the idea of "power sharing" between Marcos and Aquino: "Forget reconciliation," he said. Then Weinberger insisted that there must be new elections. Gates interceded: "Let's be realistic, not legalistic. The public view is that Aquino won. So we have to think of a way to install her in power and give Marcos a fig leaf to depart. Aquino in, Marcos out." Weinberger and Poindexter objected that Reagan would not want to be seen to be dumping Marcos. Someone suggested doing nothing. Shultz said: "There's a lot to be said for that." Habib thundered: "Give Marcos a chance to stay, and he'll hang on. He has to go!"[85] The meeting ended with an agreement to prepare public statements encouraging Marcos to leave without causing bloodshed. Shultz decided, however, that it was time to present the case for calling on Marcos to resign directly to Reagan. He determined to do it that afternoon at a meeting of the NSC, to be attended by Reagan.

Before the NSC meeting began, news came from Bosworth that Marcos was preparing to attack the rebels at daybreak--less than six hours away. Shultz prepared a sequence of actions for Reagan, involving the dispatch of Laxalt and Habib to Manila. Laxalt was to give a letter from Reagan to Marcos, urging him to resign, and Habib was to use his diplomatic skills to ensure a smooth succession.

With Reagan, Bush, Casey, and Regan in attendance, Shultz told the NSC that it was clear Marcos could no longer govern the Philippines. Weinberger agreed with Shultz. The only person present who argued for continuing to support Marcos was Donald Regan (who had not been at Shultz's house that morning). He and Habib quickly became involved in "a verbal brawl," Regan (apparently taking it on himself to speak for the president) recalling "what had happened in Iran" and protesting that the US "could not abandon Marcos." Aquino, he said, was an unknown quantity: If they abandoned Marcos, they could be "opening the door to communism."[86]

As the argument went backwards and forwards, Reagan's attention seemed to wane. When he joined in the discussion, it was essentially to outline the terms on which Marcos was to be approached. He should be invited, not told, to resign; he should be offered asylum. And the communication was to be made through normal channels: Reagan refused to call Marcos, or to send a personal message.

After the NSC meeting, the president approved a White House statement saying, "The president appealed earlier to President Marcos to avoid an attack against other elements of the Philippine armed forces." Noting that the United States was providing military assistance to the Philippines, the White House statement went on: "We cannot continue our existing military assistance if the government uses that aid against other elements of the Philippine military which enjoy substantial popular backing. The president urges in the strongest possible terms that violence be avoided as Filipinos of good will work to resolve the ongoing crisis." The emphasis on avoidance of violence reflected the White House's preoccupation with several scenarios of bloodshed, all of which might appear on evening television with proportionate damage to the president's reputation. In one, Marcos's troops would mow down Aquino's supporters; in another, Enrile's men would capture the palace and massacre Marcos and his family (evoking in Republican minds the murder of Diem in 1963).[87]

Reagan approved a message to Marcos, asking him "what his thoughts were about transitioning [sic] to a new government."[88] He offered Marcos asylum in the United States, being particularly anxious to prevent the Philippine president from becoming "another shah, left to wander from country to country, without a home, without a welcome in the United States."[89]

But when Bosworth read Reagan's statement to Marcos, the Filipino recognized it for what it was. "What do you mean I can't use force?" he asked Bosworth. "I'm the duly elected president of the Philippines. This is a military coup attempt. It's a revolution."[90] Marcos saw clearly that he was in trouble, but he had not yet decided to give up. He vowed to "fight to the last breath, even though my family cowers in terror in the palace."[91]

Bosworth then recommended to Wolfowitz that the administration should issue a statement saying the time had come for a transition to a new government. Bosworth felt strongly that the word "transition" must be in the statement. That would make it unmistakably clear to Marcos that he must go. The Department of State drafted the statement and sent it in to the NSC staff. The NSC at this point had drawn on an extensive network of advisers, including Alejandro Melchor, a former executive secretary of Marcos.[92]

Rather than conducting a heroic last stand, Marcos was desperately trying to make deals with the opposition. Throughout the Monday in Manila, Marcos tried to shore up his collapsing government, offering Enrile partnership in a coalition that would exclude Aquino. Enrile refused the offer.

At 5 a.m. on February 24, the White House got news that Marcos had ordered an attack on the rebels. The administration issued a statement that concluded: "Attempts to prolong the life of the present regime by violence are futile. A solution to this crisis can only be achieved through a peaceful transition to a new government."[93] Bosworth conveyed this statement to Marcos, and it was then made public. Meanwhile, a message was sent to Ver through an ex-CIA official asking him not to use force and offering him and his family asylum in the United States.

Still clinging to the hope that Reagan would save him, Marcos phoned Senator Laxalt on Capitol Hill and asked him to discuss with Reagan the idea of Marcos sharing power with Aquino. He suggested that he could become

Aquino's "senior adviser" while serving out his term until 1987: He was, he pointed out, experienced in fighting Communists as well as skilled in dealing with foreign creditors.[94]

Though Laxalt seemed ready to consider seriously the "power sharing" proposal, Shultz, Habib, and Armacost scorned the idea of a coalition, predicting that it would lead to civil war. Laxalt and Shultz drove to the White House, where they discovered that Imelda Marcos (who had been calling Nancy Reagan frequently during the crisis) had been on the phone to the president's wife with her own proposals for "power sharing." When Laxalt and Shultz met the president, Shultz quickly dampened any enthusiasm Laxalt still had for a coalition, rejecting the notion as "impractical."

Laxalt then phoned Marcos back to say that the president felt it would be "impractical and undignified" for Marcos to share power, but that Marcos was welcome to live in the United States. Marcos asked directly whether Reagan wanted him to resign, but Laxalt avoided giving a direct answer. Then Marcos asked Laxalt for the senator's own opinion on whether he should step down. Laxalt replied, "I think you should cut and cut cleanly. I think the time has come." Marcos replied: "I am so very, very disappointed."[95]

Despite his disappointment, Marcos went ahead and had himself formally inaugurated as president, two hours after Aquino had been inaugurated in a rival ceremony across town. Half an hour before Aquino's inauguration, Marcos called Enrile and suggested a triumvirate--a coalition consisting of Marcos, Enrile, and Aquino.

Late in the afternoon, Marcos called Enrile and told him that he was leaving. That evening, Marcos crossed the river and met Enrile, who was waiting under the trees with some RAM bodyguards. They talked for a while and finally embraced. At nine o'clock, Marcos, Ver, and their families boarded two US helicopters and flew to Clark Air Base. Watching them from the Embassy was Ambassador Bosworth, who immediately picked up a phone, called Corazon Aquino, greeting her with the words "Madame President."

Early the next morning, after hearing rumors of loyalist troops approaching Clark, the US Air Force virtually bundled the Marcoses onto a transport plane which flew them to Guam and then to exile in Hawaii.

DISCUSSION QUESTIONS

1. *Was the outcome of the Philippine crisis a "success" for American foreign policy, as was widely claimed in 1986? "Successful" in respect of what?*

2. *What were the goals of US policy? Which of them were advanced or achieved by the removal of Marcos and the manner in which it was handled by the Reagan administration?*

3. *To what extent (and in what ways) did the actions of the US administration actually contribute to the outcome?*

4. *In what ways, if any, was US policymaking itself more "successful" on this occasion than in the other cases examined? To what do you attribute this greater success?*

5. *In what ways was the Philippines problem an easier one for the US administration to deal with than the problems examined elsewhere in the book?*

6. *In what ways does the Philippines case support or refute the belief that Reagan was remote from the substance of foreign policy?*

NOTES

1. The text in this section is adapted from Donald M. Goldstein, *U.S. Policy Concerning Renewal of the Military Base Agreement with the Philippines* (Pew case no. 325), 16.

2. The events of this period are described in detail in Stanley Karnow's recent book, *In Our Image. America's Empire in the Philippines* (New York: Random House, 1989), Chapters 4 and 5.

3. The text in this section is adapted from Goldstein, *U.S. Policy Concerning Renewal*, 16-17.

4. However, their value on this level was even questionable because Congress had refused to budget enough funds to allow the navy to build up an adequate defense force on the islands.

5. The text in this section is adapted from Goldstein, *U.S. Policy Concerning Renewal*, 16-17.

6. *Ibid.*, 16-17. Karnow points out that Manila was (after Warsaw) the most damaged Allied city in World War II.

7. *Ibid.*, 18.

8. *Ibid.* Interestingly, General Dwight D. Eisenhower, who was then army chief of staff, recommended in 1946 that the US army withdraw from the islands. Eisenhower strongly believed that negotiations over basing rights would place more of a strain on Philippine-US relations than was merited in light of the bases' strategic value. Later, the escalation of the Cold War and the adoption of the containment policy changed Eisenhower's mind.

9. *Ibid.*

10. *Ibid.*, 19.

11. *Ibid.*

12. The tactical air force in the Philippines is four hours by air from Japan and Korea.

13. The text in this section is adapted from Goldstein, *U.S. Policy Concerning Renewal*, 19.

14. *Ibid.*, 20.

15. Salvador P. Lopez, "The Politics of Philippine Security," in *National Security Interests in the Pacific Basin*, ed. Claude Buss (Stanford, CA: Stanford University, Hoover Institution Press, 1985), 218.

16. The text in this section is adapted from Goldstein, *U.S. Policy Concerning Renewal*, 19.

17. *Ibid.*

18. In 1984 Brunei joined to bring ASEAN's total to six.

19. Official hagiographies of Marcos asserted (as did the president) that he had played a distinguished role as a guerrilla leader and that he had been awarded numerous medals for gallantry, including the Distinguished Service Cross, two Silver Stars, and the Congressional Medal of Honor. On the debunking of these claims, see Raymond Bonner, *Waltzing with a Dictator. The Marcoses and the Making of American Policy* (New York: Vintage Books, 1988), 14-17, 321-322, 405-406. On his actual wartime activities, see Sterling Seagrave, *The Marcos Dynasty* (New York: Harper & Row, 1988), Chapter 3.

20. Karnow, *In Our Image*, 381-382.

21. Bonner, *Waltzing with a Dictator*, 307. Another provision required that presidential candidates be at least fifty years of age: Aquino would be slightly under fifty when the first elections under the amended constitution took place.

22. *Ibid.*, 309.

23. Penelope Walker, *Political Crisis and Debt Negotiations: The Case of the Philippines* (Pew Case no. 133), 4; Karnow, *In Our Image*, 385.

24. Bonner, *Waltzing with a Dictator*, 342.

25. Aquino was certainly aware of Marcos's condition: according to some accounts, this was a major factor in his decision to return.

26. American officials differed over who was responsible for the murder of Aquino. The intelligence community concluded that the assassination, while possibly not ordered by Marcos, who was known to be incapacitated, was probably carried out by the Philippine army on his behalf and almost certainly at the direction of Ver. Ver and Imelda were thought to be concerned that Aquino would rally the many elements disenchanted with Marcos, particularly as the president's health was failing.

27. Bonner, *Waltzing with a Dictator*, 357.

28. Raymond Bonner, for example, writes: "[The embassy staff] had not realized the depth of the opposition to Marcos. It was a repeat of what had happened in Iran, where the United States had had no appreciation of the strength of the opposition to the shah and therefore failed to develop a policy that fitted reality. The cost of being so close to the dictator--American officials knew Marcos well, as their counterparts had known the shah--while

keeping their distance from opposition leaders, a distance maintained because the Marcoses were offended when American diplomats were seen with the opposition, was that embassy staff and intelligence officers had lost contact with the people they were supposed to know" (*Waltzing with a Dictator*, 346).

29. Reagan was persuaded to cancel the visit to Manila after US officials unfriendly to Marcos convinced Nancy Reagan that Manila was "a security nightmare," thus reminding her of the failed assassination attempt against the president in January 1981 (Karnow, *In Our Image*, 408).

30. Bonner, *Waltzing with a Dictator*, 355.

31. Karnow, *In Our Image*, 414.

32. Bonner, *Waltzing with a Dictator*, 355.

33. *Ibid.*, 356.

34. *Ibid*, 364, 365. The questioner was Morton Kondracke of the *New Republic*. In debating with Walter Mondale, Reagan asserted that to throw Marcos "to the wolves" would leave the United States "facing a Communist power in the Pacific" (Karnow, *In Our Image*, 408).

35. William E. Kline, *The Fall of Marcos* (Pew Case no. 439), 11.

36. An equally disconcerting report was prepared at this time by James Nach, a political officer at the embassy in Manila. Nach concluded after visiting Mindanao that there was a serious possibility of "a Communist takeover" (Bonner, *Waltzing with a Dictator*, 360; Karnow, *In Our Image*, 406-407).

37. Cited in Kline, *The Fall of Marcos*, 11.

38. William E. Kline, interview with Richard Armitage, May 17, 1988. This view of policymaking differs interestingly from that given in Bonner's *Waltzing with a Dictator*, which depicts a struggle between "the professionals in the bureaucracies" and the "ideologues in the White House." While the term *professional* could encompass both career officials and political appointees, Armitage's remarks suggest that the very success of the group to which he belonged arose partly from the exclusion of career officers and that its cohesion stemmed from the fact that its members shared a preoccupation with serving the president. In this sense, the point of view of the political appointees was different from that of career officers, though there is in fact no evidence that the two groups differed significantly on substance. Equally, both accounts agree that the core group around Reagan (whether or not they are labelled "ideologues") was the center of resistance to the movement to abandon Marcos.

39. Crowe--like Armacost--had found direct contact with the Marcos regime to be a sobering experience. After visiting Manila in June 1984, he concluded that: "Marcos was not making the decisions that had to be made, primarily because of his personal vanity. His health was a serious problem. He was concerned about his survival, his affluence and his well-being, and the country was sliding downhill. So, I felt, he had to go" (Karnow, *In Our Image*, 407). Crowe wrote to Marcos, proposing reforms, and to President Reagan himself suggesting that the United States "start right now to develop a policy

to persuade Marcos to leave office." Crowe remarked that this initiative left him as serving officer "very uneasy." As he told Karnow: "It's not comfortable to recommend to your own government that a head of state be deposed or encouraged to step down. That is a momentous step" (*ibid.*).

40. Bonner, *Waltzing with a Dictator*, 384. Crowe commented that Weinberger was "a conservative, reluctant to make changes . . . a tough man to persuade": there is no evidence that Weinberger was ever an advocate of dropping Marcos.

41. Cited in Kline, *The Fall of Marcos*, 13.

42. Bonner, *Waltzing with a Dictator*, 367.

43. William Kline, interview with Armitage, May 17, 1988.

44. Cited in Kline, *The Fall of Marcos*, 14.

45. Richard Childress argued that Reagan in fact knew all along that Marcos was "part of the problem" and that he was fully informed of all that the NSC and the State Department were doing. In his view, Reagan preferred to give Marcos time to reform: "It became a matter of timing, a matter of making sure there was a Philippine solution, that it was developed and the Filipinos could feel they carried out the revolution, not the Americans" (William E. Kline, interview with Childress, March 24, 1988).

46. Cited in Kline, *The Fall of Marcos*, 15.

47. Ambassador Bosworth later recalled broaching the subject of "revitalizing democratic institutions" with Marcos: "I could see his eyes glaze over as he heard this once more from an American ambassador" (Karnow, *In Our Image*, 409).

48. Bonner, *Waltzing with a Dictator*, 382-383.

49. *Ibid.*, 379.

50. *Ibid.*, 385. The main "former ambassador" was obviously Armacost. Imelda Marcos believed that her displeasure with Armacost had resulted in his being posted to Washington. Since he returned to take up the third most important position in the State Department, Armacost's return was hardly one shrouded in disgrace.

51. So were others. When Laxalt was about to leave for Manila, he was startled to be approached by the doughty Admiral Crowe and told simply: "Get rid of Marcos."

52. Paul Laxalt, "My Conversations with Ferdinand Marcos: A Lesson in Personal Diplomacy," *Policy Review*, Summer 1986, 2. The Laxalt mission was conceived by Wolfowitz and Bosworth, the State Department being unhappy about the failure of the reform strategy.

53. There is some disagreement about who (if not Marcos himself) conceived the idea of a snap election: see Laxalt, "My Conversations with Ferdinand Marcos"; Bonner, *Waltzing with a Dictator*, 391; Karnow, *In Our Image*, 409.

54. Bonner, *Waltzing with a Dictator*, 387.

55. Marcos took this advice, hiring the conservatively inclined firm of Black, Manafort, Stone, and Kelly, which charged him close to $1 million for its services (Karnow, *In Our Image*, 409).

56. As Bonner notes, this conviction took on an almost paranoid form: "In late October, Marcos asked aides to research the fall of Diem, Allende, the shah, Somoza, and Park Chung Hee. He instructed his researchers to study *New York Times* stories and especially editorials prior to the ouster of these men. Reflecting an anxiety bordering on paranoia, Marcos told confidants (who told Americans) that James Nach, the Embassy political officer, was a leader in the effort to destabilize his government. Marcos was sure of this because Nach had been in Vietnam--even though Nach's service in Vietnam had been many years after Diem's ouster" (*Waltzing with a Dictator*, 388-389). Ironically, the possibility of an assassination had been discussed in Washington, and at the National War College meeting in August the case of Diem had indeed come up.

57. Karnow, *In Our Image*, 410.

58. Bonner, *Waltzing with a Dictator*, 391. The announcement of a snap election also came as a surprise to the intelligence community, which had by that time come to the conclusion that Marcos would wait until the scheduled elections in 1987.

59. *Ibid.*, 393.

60. Lewis M. Simons, *Worth Dying For* (New York: William Morrow, 1987), 257-277.

61. Karnow suggests that, though Aquino was to be included in the original council to issue from the coup, "their choice for eventual president was Enrile, not Cory" (*In Our Image*, 416).

62. Laurel (described by Karnow as "a routine politician of dubious repute") was a son of Jose B. Laurel, a Filipino lawyer and nationalist who collaborated with the Japanese during the war. The son was a senator and had split from Marcos in 1980, becoming the leader of the United Democratic Nationalist Organization (UNIDO). Laurel naturally expected to be UNIDO's presidential candidate. As Cardinal Sin recognized, his history and style made him insufficiently different from Marcos to be able to attract a mass following.

63. Karnow, *In Our Image*, 411.

64. Bonner, *Waltzing with a Dictator*, 396. Cardinal Sin was acting with the full, if undeclared, assent of Ambassador Bosworth.

65. The leader of the group in the United States was Robert Trent Jones, Jr., a leading golf course designer and therefore somebody who in the course of his work tended to meet leading congressmen and officials. Indeed, it was at a club near San Francisco that Jones waylaid his old golfing partner, George Shultz, and told him of his plans for helping Aquino. According to Bonner, "a receptive Shultz told Jones to stay in touch with Armacost" (*Waltzing with a Dictator*, 401).

66. According to Seagrave (*The Marcos Dynasty*, 402), the nickname "Jukebox" was applied to Tolentino as he lost his earlier zeal for reform and came under Marcos's sway. Hence the joke in Manila--"Put a few coins in and he'll play any tune you want."

67. The statement was drafted in the State Department and endorsed by the NSC and the Department of Defense.

68. Bonner, *Waltzing with a Dictator*, 408.

69. Quoted in *Ibid.*, 410. Conservatives also relied on an article in *Commentary* that depicted the NPA as a brutal and ruthless organization: see Ross H. Munro, "The New Khmer Rouge," *Commentary* 80 (December 1985), 19-38.

70. NAMFREL was partly financed by the US government: Roughly $1 million was fed to it through the National Endowment for Democracy, a body set up by the Reagan administration to promote the American way of life and politics abroad. The United States also provided money for Radio Veritas, the Catholic-owned opposition radio station in the Philippines.

71. There were serious tensions within the group, between the conservatives nominated by the White House, who wanted to emphasize the more positive aspects of the election, and liberals, such as Senator John F. Kerry (D-MA), who were determined to expose the full scale of the fraud that they had observed.

72. Kline, *The Fall of Marcos*, 21.

73. Karnow, *In Our Image*, 414.

74. Most sources agree both that this was Aquino's fear and that it was not Habib's intention. For a different version, see Seagrave, *The Marcos Dynasty*, 406-407.

75. Some of Aquino's suspicion was due to the fact that the American media had stressed Habib's recent efforts to create a coalition government in Lebanon: She assumed that his mission in the Philippines would be the same.

76. Karnow, *In Our Image*, 415.

77. Kline, *The Fall of Marcos*, 21. In the same conference, Reagan stressed his preoccupation with the bases: "I don't know of anything more important than those bases," he declared.

78. Bosworth described the twenty-four hours following the press conference as "probably the single worst day of my life" (Karnow, *In Our Image*, 414).

79. Until the very end, White House statements referred to fraud as being committed by "the ruling party," not by Marcos.

80. According to Karnow, both Ver and Bosworth were already aware of RAM's intentions. This was hardly surprising, since the plotters tended to do their plotting over drinks at a large hotel in Manila.

81. Since Filipinos, as well as American critics, have tended to see American hands at work in Philippine politics, there was speculation that the United States had pushed Enrile and Ramos into open rebellion. But even Bonner,

who tends to emphasize American overt and covert involvement, believes that there was no official encouragement, if only because the White House was still clinging to the possibility of saving Marcos.

82. Karnow, *In Our Image*, 418.

83. *Ibid.*, 419.

84. The following section draws heavily on the account in Karnow, *In Our Image*, 419. A similar but much briefer account appears in Bonner, *Waltzing with a Dictator*, 442.

85. Karnow, *In Our Image*, 419.

86. The Regan-Habib argument is described in Bonner, *Waltzing with a Dictator*, 442, and Karnow, *In Our Image*, 420.

87. Karnow, *In Our Image*, 420.

88. Seagrave, *The Marcos Dynasty*, 414.

89. Bonner, *Waltzing with a Dictator*, 443; Karnow, *In Our Image*, 420.

90. William Kline, interview with Bosworth, March 9, 1988.

91. Karnow, *In Our Image*, 421.

92. Melchor spent the last forty-eight hours of the Marcos regime ensconced in the situation room at the White House, telling the Americans "which buttons to push" to get Marcos to resign.

93. Karnow, *In Our Image*, 421.

94. Marcos also asked Reagan if he would provide US Air Force transports to rescue him from the palace and take him up to the Ilocos, where he would raise forces against Enrile and Ramos.

95. Laxalt, "My Conversations with Ferdinand Marcos," 2.

FURTHER READING ON THE PHILIPPINES

Books

Bonner, Raymond. *Waltzing with a Dictator. The Marcoses and the Making of Foreign Policy*. New York: Vintage Books, 1988.

Karnow, Stanley. *In Our Image. America's Empire in the Philippines*. New York: Random House, 1989.

Karnow, Stanley. *In Our Image. America's Empire in the Philippines*. New York: Foreign Policy Association, 1989. Headline Series pamphlet, no. 288 (Extracts from the above.)

Marcos, Ferdinand E. *The Democratic Revolution in the Philippines* (2nd ed). Englewood Cliffs, NJ: Prentice-Hall International, 1982.

Seagrave, Sterling. *The Marcos Dynasty*. New York: Harper and Row, 1988.
Simons, Lewis M. *Worth Dying For*. New York: William Morrow, 1987.
Steinberg, David Joel. *The Philippines: A Singular and a Plural Place*. Boulder, CO: Westview Press, 1982.

Articles

Aquino, Benigno. "What's Wrong with the Philippines?" *Foreign Affairs* 46, 4 (July 1968): 770-779.
Brown, Mark Malloch. "Aquino, Marcos and the White House." *Granta* 18 (Spring 1986): 160-169.
Fallows, James. "A Damaged Culture." *Atlantic Monthly*, November 1987, 49-58.
Laxalt, Paul. "My Conversations with Ferdinand Marcos: A Lesson in Personal Diplomacy." *Policy Review*, Summer 1986, 2.
Lopez, Salvador P. "The Politics of Philippine Security." In *National Security Interests in the Pacific Basin*, ed. Claude Buss. Stanford, CA: Stanford University, Hoover Institution Press, 1985.
Manning, Robert A. "The Philippines in Crisis." *Foreign Affairs* 63 (Winter 1984), 392-410.
Munro, Ross H. "The New Khmer Rouge." *Commentary* 80, December 1985, 19-38.
Sullivan, William H. "Living without Marcos." *Foreign Policy* 53 (Winter 1983-84), 150. (Sullivan was US ambassador to Philippines from 1973-1977, when he was posted to Iran.)

ABOUT THE BOOK
AND EDITOR

For U.S. policymakers, the collapse of governments headed by "good friends of the United States" has been, over the past thirty years, a repeated cause of alarm and embarrassment. Such crises of succession have implications not only for U.S. foreign policy but also for recent and forthcoming changes in Eastern Europe and the Soviet Union.

Martin Staniland draws together extended case studies illustrating regime change and shows how each crisis resembles the others in its phases of development—from the status quo to the "attack" phase and, ultimately, to negotiating the succession. In the process, students get to know the history, culture, and personalities involved from Batista and Eisenhower to Marcos and the Reagan administration.

As in every volume in the *Case Studies in International Affairs* series, this volume opens with an introduction that taps into current theoretical debates in international relations while giving students a framework for understanding and comparing the cases that follow. Individual introductions to each case place the study in context, and discussion questions and exercises are strategically interjected throughout to encourage students to explore the issues and to assess the choices facing policymakers.

Martin Staniland is a professor in the Graduate School of Public and International Affairs at the University of Pittsburgh.

DATE DUE

FEB 17 93			

Falling   227354